Virtue and Reality

MAY THE BUDDHADHARMA REACH ALL SENTIENT BEINGS · LAMA YESHE WISDOM ARCHIVE

Previously published by the LAMA YESHE WISDOM ARCHIVE

Becoming Your Own Therapist, by Lama Yeshe
Advice for Monks and Nuns, by Lama Yeshe and Lama Zopa Rinpoche
Make Your Mind an Ocean, by Lama Yeshe
Teachings from the Vajrasattva Retreat, by Lama Zopa Rinpoche

For initiates only:
A Chat about Heruka, by Lama Zopa Rinpoche
A Chat about Yamantaka, by Lama Zopa Rinpoche

Forthcoming in 2000
Making Life Meaningful, by Lama Zopa Rinpoche
*The Essence of Tibetan Buddhism: The Three Principal Aspects of the Path
and An Introduction to Tantra,* by Lama Yeshe

(Contact us for information)

*May whoever sees, touches, reads, remembers, or talks or thinks about these
booklets never be reborn in unfortunate circumstances, receive only rebirths
in situations conducive to the perfect practice of Dharma, meet only perfectly
qualified spiritual guides, quickly develop bodhicitta and immediately
attain enlightenment for the sake of all sentient beings.*

LAMA ZOPA RINPOCHE

VIRTUE AND REALITY

Method and Wisdom in the Practice of Dharma

Edited by Nicholas Ribush

LAMA YESHE WISDOM ARCHIVE • BOSTON

www.LamaYeshe.com

A non-profit charitable organization for the benefit of all
sentient beings and a section of the Foundation for the
Preservation of the Mahayana Tradition
www.fpmt.org

First published 1998
5,000 copies for free distribution
Second printing 2000, 10,000

LAMA YESHE WISDOM ARCHIVE
PO BOX 356
WESTON
MA 02493 USA

ISBN 1-891868-02-0

10 9 8 7 6 5 4 3 2

Front cover photograph by Ven. Roger Kunsang

Printed in Canada on recycled, acid-free paper

Please contact the LAMA YESHE WISDOM ARCHIVE for copies of our free booklets

CONTENTS

Publisher's Acknowledgments

We are extremely grateful to our friends and supporters who have made it possible for the LAMA YESHE WISDOM ARCHIVE to both exist and function. To Lama Yeshe and Lama Zopa Rinpoche, whose kindness is impossible to repay. To Peter and Nicole Kedge and Venerable Ailsa Cameron for helping bring the ARCHIVE to its present state of development. To Venerable Roger Kunsang, Lama Zopa's tireless assistant, for his kindness and consideration. And to our sustaining supporters: Drs. Penny Noyce & Leo Liu, Barry & Connie Hershey, Joan Terry, Roger & Claire Ash-Wheeler, Henry & Catherine Lau, Claire Atkins, Ecie Hursthouse, Lily Chang Wu, Nancy Pan, Thubten Yeshe Alexander, Therese Miller, Tom & Suzanne Castles, Datuk Tai Tsu Kuang, Chuah Kok Leng, the Caytons (Lori, Karuna, Pam, Bob & Amy), Claire Ritter, Tom Thorning, Wisdom Books (London), Tan Swee Eng, Salim Lee, Richard Gere, Cecily Drucker, Lynnea Elkind, Janet Moore, Su Hung and Carol Davies.

We are also grateful to Jane Harmon Hein for her most excellent donation, which helped cover many of the costs of reprinting this booklet.

We are also indebted to those generous contributors who responded to the request for funds we made in our last mailing, October, 1999. Therefore, a huge thank you to Diana Abrashkin, Harmony Adkins, Dean Alper, Ben & Deb Alterman, Margie Amick, Amitabha Buddhist Centre, Anne Amos, Leticia Anson, Ruben Anton, Steve Armstrong, Isabel Arocena, Charlotte Avant, Faith Bach, Luke Bailey, Peter Baker, Judi Beardsley, Kerstin Beck, David Bellos, Jacalyn Bennett, Peggy Bennington, Bradley Black, Allan Bomhard, Andrew Bordwin, Siliana Bosa (for the good rebirth of Vincenzo Grazioli),

Betsy Bourdon, Robyn Brentano & Bill Kelley, Robert & Anne Britton, René & Marguerite Brochard, Ross Brooke, Don Brown, Pamela Butler, Claudia Callan, Jennifer Campanelli, Mark Campbell, Felix Carabello, Margaret Carmier, Laura Carter, Steve & Polly Casmar, Chandrakirti Meditation Centre, Vicki Chen, June Cheng, Thubten Chönyid, Ngawang Chötak, Robin Coleman, Gavriella Conn, Bryan Cooper, Doug Crane & Deje Zhoga, Eleanor Cusick, Maryann Czermak, Daniel De Biasi, Nan Deal, Ricardo de Aratanha, Linda de Witt & Robert Green, Laure Dillon, Cecily Drucker, John Dunne & Sara McClintock, Ken & Malou Dusyn, Joseph Dynh, Dzogchen Foundation, Keith Emmons, Adam Engle, Donna Estess, Richard Farris, Adriana Ferranti, Ven. René Feusi, Martha Foster, Sesame Fowler, Terry Fralich & Rebecca Wing, Claudia Frey, Robert & Sheryl Friedman, Marianne Fritz, Lynn Gebetsberger, Eileen Gebrian, Nancy Gibson, Kathleen Glomski, Julio Gonzalez, Judy & Ian Green, Sandy Grindlay, Worth Gurkin, Lucile Hamlin, Bernard Handler, Wyatt Harlan, Margi Haas, Richard Hay, Graziella Heins, Myron Helmer, Christine Hether, W. Bosco Ho, Lisa Hochman, Larry Howe & Martha Tack, Ken Huber, Victoria Huckenpahler, Walter Illes, Elaine Jackson, James Johns, Ven. Tenzin Kachö, Toni Kenyon, Eric Klaft, Nicholas Kolivas, Camille Kozlowski, Lorne & Terry Ladner, Mim Lagoe, Tony Lagreca, Chiu Mei Lai, Ven. Chiu Min Lai, Chiu Nan Lai, Laurence Laubsher, Alfred Leyens, Ven. Trime Lhamo, John Liberty, Li Lightfoot, Judy Lin, Ludovico Lopez Cadé, Sue Lucksted-Tharp, Kendall Magnussen, Beth Magura, John & Barbara Makransky, Lenard Martin, Doss McDavid, Diego Melendez, Menkit, Elea & Michael Mideke, Amy Miller, Lynda Millspaugh, Zbigniew Modrzejewski, Marilyn Montgomery, Theobold Mordey, Paula Moreau, Jack Morison, Kalleen Mortensen, Dolores Moses, Ada Mundo, Steve Nahaczewski, Stacy O'Leary, Ann Parker, Michele Paterson, David Patt, Dennis Paulson, Justin Pollard, Jacek Pollner, Ellen Powell, George Propps, Janyce Reidel, Leslie Reincke, Isabel Resano, Mariette Risley, John Ross, Carol Royce-Wilder, Elaine Rysner, Jesse Sartain, Priscilla Sawa, Robert Schense, Victoria Scott, Brian Selius, Jhampa Shaneman, Rosa Shen, Kim Shetter, Susan Shore, Beth Simon, Yolanda Snell, Lynne Sonenberg, Nova Spivak, Elin Steinthorsdottir, Kay Stewart, Hans & Helga

Steyskal, Sarah Stiles, Dawn Stracener, Susan Stumpf, Laurie Sulzer, Lana Sundberg, Sandra Tatlock, Debra Thornburg, Thubten Kunga Center, Jessica Torres, Ven. Charles Trebaol, Wendy vanden Heuvel, Barbara Vautier, Chris Vautier, Lynn Wade, Tom Waggoner, Shasta Wallace, Sylvia Wasek, Lila & Joel Weinberg, Matthew Weiss, Judith Weitzner, Jane Werner, Kate Lila Wheeler, Bonda White, Cat Wilson, Loren Wilson, Louie Bob Wood, Soo Hwa Yeo and Ven. Sarah Tenzin Yiwong.

Finally, we would also like to thank the many kind people who have asked that their donations be kept anonymous and the volunteers who have given so generously of their time to help us with our mailings.

If you, dear reader, would like to join this noble group of open-hearted altruists by contributing to the production of more free booklets by Lama Yeshe or Lama Zopa Rinpoche or to any other aspect of the LAMA YESHE WISDOM ARCHIVE'S work, please contact us to find out how.

This book is published in honor of Lama Zopa Rinpoche's visit to Boston, November 1998. We would like to thank the members of Tilopa Center for organizing and taping these teachings, Venerable Roger Kunsang for suggesting that we publish them, Venerable Thubten Munsel for transcribing the tapes, Peter Iseli for our beauti-fully drawn logo, Wendy Cook and Linda Gatter for their editorial suggestions and Mark Gatter for his help in the design and production of this book.

Through the merit of having contributed to the spread of the Buddha's teachings for the sake of all sentient beings, may our benefactors and their families and friends have long and healthy lives, all happiness, and may all their Dharma wishes be instantly fulfilled.

EDITOR'S INTRODUCTION

The entire Dharma, the teachings of the Buddha, can be divided into two categories—extensive method and profound wisdom. The method lineage passed from Shakyamuni Buddha to Maitreya and down through the great Indian pundits such as Asanga, Vasubandhu, Haribhadra and Suvarnadvipi to the great Atisha, who brought them to Tibet. Similarly, the wisdom lineage passed from the Buddha to Manjushri and again down to Atisha through pundits such as Nagarjuna and Chandrakirti.

In Tibet, Atisha arranged the Buddha's teachings into a graded sequence that became known as the steps of the path to enlightenment (*lam-rim*), the essence of which is method and wisdom. Explicitly, this path has three principal aspects—renunciation, bodhicitta and right view. The Kadampa tradition, founded by Atisha, became the basis of the Gelug school of Tibetan Buddhism, which itself was founded in the fifteenth century by the enlightened scholar and yogi, Lama Je Tsong Khapa. This tradition lives today in the minds and teachings of great masters such as His Holiness the Dalai Lama and other wonderful teachers in the Gelug tradition, of whom Lama Thubten Zopa Rinpoche, the author of this book, is one of the best known. He is the spiritual director of the Foundation for the Preservation of the Mahayana Tradition (FPMT) and the guide, refuge and protector of thousands of students all over the world.

In the context of the teachings presented here, method is the loving, compassionate bodhicitta and wisdom is the realization of ultimate reality, the right view of emptiness. It would be hard to find a simpler, clearer, more practical explanation of these two fundamental paths than the one Lama Zopa offers us here. Through practicing method, we attain the holy body of a Buddha; through developing wisdom we attain the enlightened mind.

Based on a four-day course given at an American FPMT center, Tilopa Center, Decatur, Illinois, in August, 1997, the teachings presented here detail methods for developing compassion and wisdom in our everyday lives. Recognizing the workaday world reality in which most of his students live, Rinpoche shows us how to think and act so that every moment of our lives will be of maximum benefit to both ourselves and others. What more do we need?

FULFILLING LIFE'S PURPOSE

How can we make best use of this perfect human rebirth, the precious human body that we have received just this once? How can we make it most beneficial, not only for ourselves but for those other, most precious, extremely important living beings? Just like us, numberless other living beings, each of whom is as equally precious as we feel ourselves to be, seek only happiness and dislike any suffering. How can we make our lives productive for their sake? This is the main thing we should be asking ourselves.

If we take care of others, work for their happiness, we are automatically taking care of ourselves. Trying to make others happy is the best way of loving ourselves. Similarly, if we harm others, we harm ourselves. Harming others does not bring us peace and happiness, only misery and grief, now and in the future. Bringing happiness to others is the best way of bringing happiness to ourselves; it follows naturally. It happens by the way. Things we do that bring happiness to others have a beneficial effect on our own minds.

Conversely, if we act toward others with negative motivation and give them harm, such actions leave negative imprints on our mental continuum. These imprints later manifest as undesirable appearances. When our senses come into contact with these, unpleasant feelings arise. This is the evolution of our life's problems; this is how they start. Their origin is in our own minds, with our negative thoughts. The end result is the suffering we experience, in this life or in future ones.

Healthy actions—positive actions, actions that benefit others, actions done with compassion, with sincerity, which bring happiness to others—leave positive imprints on our mental continuum. These manifest as desirable appearances. When our senses contact these, pleasant feelings, comfort, success—all the enjoyable experiences we wish for and desire—result. This is the evolution of happiness, all the way up to enlightenment. Happy daily lives, pleasure and enjoyment—from now until enlightenment—result from positive thinking, positive intention, positive actions.

That's why the Buddha of Compassion, His Holiness the Dalai Lama, often says that cherishing others is the best way of cherishing ourselves. His Holiness calls this wise, or intelligent, selfishness because, as I mentioned above, by cherishing others, refraining from giving them harm, offering them all benefit, all our wishes for happiness, both now and in the future, will be fulfilled. Experience has proven that not only temporary happiness, but even enlightenment, the ultimate state of everlasting happiness, the highest, complete attainment of peace and bliss, results from serving others. In fact, the more we dedicate ourselves to others, the quicker and easier our own happiness arises. This is the natural evolution of happiness.

This means living a life of compassion. Therefore, the answer to the question of how to make best use of our life is by living with compassion and wisdom. Compassion alone is not enough. We also need to develop wisdom. How do we develop wisdom? We don't get wisdom from pills or a special diet or by transplanting somebody else's brain into our head or someone's heart into our chest. We can develop wisdom only through our own effort, our own meditation practice. Wisdom comes from listening to the right teachings and reflecting and meditating on them.

Therefore, we need to receive unmistaken teachings, gain unmistaken understanding, perform unmistaken practice and thus attain unmistaken realizations. This is extremely important. In this way we do not waste our lives, don't get led along the wrong path, and can realize the potential of our lives, which is as limitless as the sky. All living beings wish only happiness and complete freedom from suffering. The purpose of our lives is to benefit them all, as extensively as possible.

Furthermore, we must learn how to analyze and meditate. As simply reading a prescription cannot cure a disease—one needs to take the medicine—mere intellectual understanding of the teachings is not enough. We have to practice.

In order to put an end to all our suffering, the cycle of old age, sickness, death and rebirth and the problems of the intermediate state as well, we need to cure our sick minds, to make a complete recovery from the mental illness—the disturbing emotional thoughts, the delusions—that causes all these unwanted experiences. For our own ultimate peace, let alone that of others, we have to do this.

We have enjoyed temporary happiness numberless times. There's not a single new temporary happiness left for us to experience. What *is* new, what we have never before experienced, is the great peace that results from cessation of all suffering, death and rebirth; the ultimate happiness that arises through complete cessation of the true cause of suffering—ignorance, the disturbing, emotional thoughts and the actions motivated by these unhealthy minds. We have never experienced this before.

Since beginningless time we have been forced to circle through the realms of death and rebirth again and again, repeatedly experiencing the whole samsaric package of life problems, the entire collection, over and over again. We have never experienced the end of this, ultimate, everlasting happiness, the complete cessation of all problems and their cause, our own disturbing thoughts and the actions that they motivate, karma.

And achieving this great result, which we attain by actualizing the steps of the path, is just a one-time job. Once we realize everlasting happiness, the cessation of all suffering, we can never suffer again, because the seed of life's problems, which we have planted in our mental continuum, has been totally eradicated, completely purified. Therefore, it's impossible to ever suffer again—there's no reason, no cause. Once we have followed the path to its end, we won't ever have to do it again, we won't have to keep on practicing. Once we attain the goal, it lasts for ever. Consequently, dedicating your life to this is extremely important. It is the most worthwhile thing you can do with your life.

There's a Tibetan text, *The Three Principal Aspects of the Path*, written by the great teacher Lama Tsong Khapa, which encapsulates the three essential aspects of the path to enlightenment as taught by the Buddha—renunciation, bodhicitta and right view. These paths lead to liberation, everlasting happiness, complete freedom from the suffering realms of cyclic existence, samsara. Their practice cuts the root of all suffering, ignorance, the unknowing mind, and brings the peerless bliss of enlightenment.

Lama Tsong Khapa was a great enlightened being, a manifestation of Manjushri, the Buddha of Wisdom, the embodiment of the wisdom of all buddhas. His ocean of good qualities was as limitless as the sky, his holy mind was complete in all realizations—perfect understanding, compassion and power—and he offered infinite benefit to all sentient beings and to the teachings of the Buddha.

ORAL TRANSMISSION

It is good to receive the oral transmission of texts such as *The Three Principal Aspects,* which contains the quintessential teachings of Guru Shakyamuni Buddha. When you do, you receive the blessings of an unbroken lineage of teachings that reaches back to the great Lama Tsong Khapa himself, and imprint your mind with the steps of the entire path to enlightenment. I myself have received it from many of my own gurus, such as His Holiness the Dalai Lama and his own teachers, who themselves are enlightened beings, accomplished scholars, and, even to the ordinary view, great yogis. Because of these blessings, when you read, study and meditate on texts whose oral transmission you have received, these activities become much more effective, much more beneficial for your mind. Also, when you teach them to others, your teachings are more beneficial for their minds.

For example, Guru Shakyamuni Buddha once gave teachings to 500 swans in a field. As a result of just hearing the words, they were all reborn human in their next life, became fully ordained sangha and attained superior status as *arya* beings. They actualized the transcendent path that directly realizes the ultimate nature, thereby ceasing all delusions, all emotional thoughts, and brought to an end all suffering and its cause. Thus, simply hearing Dharma teachings can have an extremely beneficial effect on the mental continuum, even that of an animal, such that one is not only reborn human, but is able to achieve high realizations of the path, such as those of the right-seeing path.

The great Indian pundit, Vasubandhu, who composed the important text, the *Abhidharmakosha,* would recite it aloud every day. A pigeon that nested on the roof of his house used to hear him, and when it died, Vasubandhu used his clairvoyance to see where the pigeon was reborn. He discovered that it had taken rebirth as a baby boy to a family down the road, and they agreed to put their son in the highly respected pundit's care. The child—later known as Lobpön Loden (Acharya Sthiramati; Lodrö Denpa)—took ordination as a monk, became a great expert in the *Abhidharmakosha,* which he had heard so many times in his previous life as a pigeon, and wrote several commentaries on it. This is another example of the great benefit that simply hearing Dharma teachings can bring.

One of my gurus told me another story about Lobpön Loden. Just as Christians pray to the Virgin Mary, so too do many Buddhist have great faith in Tara, a female emanation of the enlightened mind. When Lobpön Loden was a child he used to try to make food offerings to a Tara statue that was kept in a glass-fronted cabinet, but every time he pushed the food up against the glass, it would fall down and he'd cry. Undaunted, because of his great devotion, he kept trying, but the food would always fall. Eventually, Tara, moved by his sincerity, caused his offerings to remain suspended, defying gravity, on the glass.

UNIVERSAL RESPONSIBILITY

The purpose of our life is not simply to solve our own problems, to gain happiness for ourselves. The purpose of our life is to be of use to others, to benefit other sentient beings, whether it be one or many. However, the real reason we're alive is to free the numberless other sentient beings from suffering and lead them to the unsurpassed happiness of full enlightenment. That is the meaning of our life. Each of us has this universal responsibility to bring the greatest happiness to all sentient beings.

How is it that we have this responsibility? If you generate compassion in your mind, you will not harm others. Peace and happiness is the absence of harm. By not harming others, you are offering them happiness and peace. Not only that, but by having compassion, you also benefit them in a more active way. The greater your compassion, the more you help other sentient beings. So all this peace and happiness that others experience as a result of your compassion has come from you, depends upon you. It is in your hands, because it is up to you whether or not you generate compassion towards others. If you do not, they do not receive the peace and happiness you have to offer; if you do, they receive all this peace and happiness from you. Therefore, you have the universal responsibility of bringing peace and happiness to each and every sentient being.

Pause here for a moment, stop reading, and meditate on the feeling of universal responsibility as I've just explained it—that if you have compassion for all living beings, each one receives great peace and happiness from you; each one receives no harm. Think, "All this peace and happiness that they experience and enjoy depends upon me." Think of the reasons for this and keep them in mind as you try to *feel* universal responsibility for all sentient beings' peace and happiness.

Meditate on the thought, "I am responsible for all sentient beings' peace and happiness."

It would be wonderful if you could practice mindfulness of this in your everyday life. Even if you cannot do many other practices—mantra recitation, sadhanas of deities, various other preliminary practices—if you can just keep in mind that the purpose of life is to bring happiness to all sentient beings and feel responsible for this, if you can maintain this attitude, remembering it again and again, you will give your life great meaning and naturally, automatically, benefit others in this way.

If you can maintain mindfulness of universal responsibility, everything you do—walking, sitting, sleeping, working, talking, eating, whatever actions you engage in—will be transformed by this positive attitude. Every action of your body, speech and mind will immediately become service for other sentient beings. When you sleep, you sleep for others; when you eat, you eat for others; when you work, you work for others; when you talk, you are talking to benefit others, to bring them happiness. The moment your attitude changes in this way, whatever you do becomes an action that benefits others.

An hour, a minute before you changed, you were acting out of ego and self-centeredness, and whatever you were doing was impure and not a cause of achieving enlightenment. Because you were motivated by ego, attachment ruled your mind and your actions did not become a cause for everlasting happiness, liberation from samsara—the six realms of suffering and their cause. They did not even become a cause for a good rebirth or happiness beyond this life. Since your actions were done out of ego and attachment, clinging to this life, they became only the cause of suffering.

But as soon as you generate the thought, "I'm responsible for all sentient beings' happiness; this is what my life's about," and feel this universal responsibility, suddenly, whatever you're doing completely transforms. It becomes work for others. It becomes healthy. It becomes a pure action unstained by ego. It becomes Dharma. Your actions become Dharma; this is the best meditation you can do. While you are working, you are meditating. While you are studying, you are meditating. No matter what you are doing, you are meditating. There's no separation between your life and meditation; your whole life becomes your practice of meditation.

If you can just keep your mind focused in this way, even though you cannot do many other practices, this positive attitude, the thought of benefiting others, converts everything you do into the best kind of Dharma, the best cause of happiness. Everything you do becomes a cause for happiness and enlightenment. Your entire daily life brings you closer and closer to the ultimate freedom of buddhahood.

If there's no compassion in your heart, what you're left with is ego, the self-centered mind. That means your entire life is dedicated to your own happiness. But what about others? They also want to be happy. You're not the only one who needs happiness; others also need happiness. Therefore, when you're under the influence of ego, it's very easy to clash with others in your daily life. You can see how the self-centered mind causes problems, difficulty getting along with others, disharmony and so forth. The stronger your ego, the more problems in your life. Other people find it difficult to be with you. Even if you find a friend, sooner or later—as your ego generates attachment and that causes anger to arise—your ego and those other emotions will make your friend an enemy.

As long as you act out of ego, you harm others, because your ego is intent on achieving happiness for yourself at the expense of others. Because of ego, other discriminating thoughts, such as anger and jealousy, arise. They produce negative actions, which cause you to harm other sentient beings. As you go from life to life with ego and the other emotional discriminating thoughts, you continually hurt others, and all sentient beings receive harm from the one person, you.

But if you generate compassion, all sentient beings receive peace and happiness from the same one person, you. If all sentient beings get angry at you and harm or even kill you, you are just one person. But if that one person, you, doesn't practice compassion, the good heart, numberless other sentient beings are at risk of being harmed by you—there's the great risk that the one person, you, will harm numberless others. Therefore, whether other people practice compassion or not, first you should do so. Develop the good heart.

LIVING WITH BODHICITTA

Again, take a break from reading and meditate on the meaning of life, the purpose of being alive.

Think, "The purpose of my life is not simply to get happiness for myself, not just to solve my own problems. The meaning of my life is to free all sentient beings from suffering and lead them to all happiness because it is from the numberless, precious sentient beings that I receive all my past, present and future happiness, temporary and ultimate, from each everyday comfort and pleasure up to the highest enlightenment." Feel this in your heart.

When you meditate on all sentient beings, start with the precious sentient beings around you right now. Start with the ones you encounter in everyday life—those in the same room, in the same building, your family, your work mates—and slowly extend your awareness beyond them to gradually encompass all sentient beings throughout infinite space. Generate the wish to free them from all suffering and its cause and bring them all happiness, without discrimination or exception. With all this in mind, think, "This is the meaning of my life; this is the reason I'm alive." Feel it.

Now think, "I, myself alone, am responsible for bringing happiness to all sentient beings and freeing them from all suffering and its cause. I am personally responsible for the happiness of each and every sentient being." Dwell with your mind in this state of universal responsibility.

Remember, too, that this responsibility extends far beyond only human beings. There are many different kinds of living being. There are numberless animals that are suffering; numberless hell beings that are suffering; numberless hungry ghosts that are suffering. There are numberless suras and asuras, those worldly gods, that are suffering. There are numberless intermediate state beings that are suffering, experiencing much fear between death and rebirth because of the terrifying appearances their karma creates. Rest your mind in the awareness that, "I am responsible to bring happiness to these numberless, precious sentient beings, the source of all my past, present and future happiness."

Now think, "The happiness of all these sentient beings—temporary, ultimate and the peerless happiness of full enlightenment—depends on whether or not I have compassion, loving kindness, the good heart. Therefore, I need to develop the method of compassion, the good heart, within me. I also need to develop wisdom. Therefore, I am going to purify my mind, accumulate merit and plant the seed of enlightenment by meditating on the path to enlightenment—not just for my own sake but for the sole purpose of bringing all happiness to the most precious, numberless sentient beings, whose value far exceeds that of countless wish-fulfilling jewels."

You can use this meditation to set your motivation before any virtuous activity—reading Dharma books, practicing meditation, listening to teachings—taking the above paragraph as an example.

Now bring your attention to the reality of your life, which is impermanent in nature and rapidly approaching death. Then think about the nature of phenomena, which although appearing to exist from their own side are, in fact, completely *empty* of existence from their own side. Not even a single atom exists from its own side. Everything is empty—your self, actions, objects—nothing exists from its own side. They do exist, but not from their own side. Whatever exists is merely labeled by the mind. Whatever functions does so merely in name. Focus your attention on this empty nature of phenomena.

If you can practice mindfulness of the facts of life—impermanence, impending death, emptiness and so forth—in your daily life, if you can maintain constant awareness of the basic nature of phenomena, you will be able to stop disturbing, emotional thoughts from arising. Normally, these disturbing thoughts control our lives, torture us daily, always give us trouble and prevent our minds from experiencing any peace. Instead of peace, happiness and satisfaction, all we get from them is dissatisfaction, unhappiness and problems—not only in this life but, through the karma they force us to create, in many future lives to come.

Thus, practicing mindfulness of impermanence, death and emptiness—the fundamental nature of phenomena, which cuts the root of suffering, ignorance, the unknowing mind—everything we do in our lives becomes the cause of our liberation from all suffering and its cause. In this way, we can help others at a deeper level by also liberating them from the cycle of death and rebirth and its cause, the disturbing thoughts and the actions they motivate, karma.

In the previous chapter I mentioned some of the benefits of receiving oral transmissions of lam-rim, or steps of the path, texts, where you imprint your mind with the entire path to enlightenment. Another very important text is the *Heart Sutra,* or the *Essence of Wisdom,* which is the heart, or essence, of the entire sutra and tantra teachings of the Buddha. This text explains transcendent wisdom, the wisdom gone beyond. The subject is emptiness, the ultimate nature of the I, the aggregates and all other phenomena. It is the essential teaching, or meditation practice, for cutting the root of samsara and attaining liberation from suffering. By receiving the blessings of the oral transmission of this text, you plant in your mental continuum the seeds to understand and realize this crucial topic, emptiness, the only direct remedy to the cause of all suffering—delusion and karma.

When you receive an oral transmission, it is important to think, "May I immediately be able to actualize in my mental continuum the meaning of every word that I hear, may every word I hear benefit all sentient beings, and when I repeat these words myself, may the path that they contain be actualized immediately in the mind of any sentient being that hears me say them." By generating this kind of motivation and listening intently to the transmission, every single word you hear will greatly benefit both yourself and all other sentient beings.

THE THREE PRINCIPAL ASPECTS OF THE PATH

Now I'm going to read an English translation of Lama Tsong Khapa's *Three Principal Aspects of the Path to Enlightenment* in order to plant the seeds of the entire path to enlightenment in our mental continuum. Short lam-rim texts like this are very important. It doesn't take long to read them, but they leave an imprint of the whole path, and these imprints become the foundation for the development of our mind to its ultimate potential. When you read such texts mindfully or listen carefully to them being read straight through, it becomes what is called direct meditation on the path to enlightenment.

Prostration to the Venerable Gurus.

I will explain to the extent that I am able
The essence of all the teachings of the Conqueror,
The path praised by the Conqueror's holy children,
The entrance for the fortunate ones who desire liberation.

Listen with clear minds, you fortunate ones,
Who rely on the path that pleases the Conqueror,
Strive to make your freedoms and endowments meaningful,
And are unattached to the pleasures of cyclic existence.

Embodied beings are bound by the longing for existence.
Without pure renunciation, there are no means to pacify

The aspiration for pleasant results in the ocean of existence.
Therefore, at the beginning, seek renunciation.
Counteract clinging to this life by familiarizing your mind
With the difficulty of finding the freedoms and endowments
And with the fleeting nature of this life.
Counteract clinging to future lives by repeatedly contemplating
The infallibility of action and result
And the sufferings of cyclic existence.

By familiarizing yourself in this way,
When you do not desire the perfections of samsara
for even an instant
And continually aspire for liberation, day and night,
At that time, you have developed renunciation.
However, renunciation without pure bodhicitta
Cannot result in the perfect happiness
of unsurpassed enlightenment.
Therefore, the wise generate the supreme mind of enlightenment.

Swept away by the four torrential rivers,
Bound by the tight bonds of actions, so difficult to escape,
Caught in the iron net of self-grasping,
Totally enveloped by the thick darkness of ignorance,
Born and reborn in boundless existence,
Incessantly tormented by the three sufferings—
Reflecting upon this state of all beings, your mothers,
Generate the supreme mind of enlightenment.

Even though you familiarize yourself with renunciation
And the mind of enlightenment,
Without the wisdom realizing emptiness,
You cannot cut the root of existence.
Therefore, strive to realize dependent arising.

Whosoever sees the infallibility of cause and result
Of all phenomena in samsara and nirvana
And destroys all modes of apprehension
Enters the path that pleases the Buddha.
Appearances are infallible dependent arisings;
Emptiness is free from assertions—
As long as these two are understood as separate,
You have not yet realized the thought of the Conqueror.
When these two realizations are simultaneous and not alternating,
The mere sight of infallible dependent arising
Brings the certainty that destroys all modes of
apprehending objects.
Then, your analysis of the profound view is complete.

Furthermore, appearances eliminate the extreme of existence
And emptiness eliminates the extreme of non-existence.
When you understand the way emptiness appears as
cause and result,
You will not be carried away by extreme views.

When you have realized the essentials
Of the three principal aspects of the path,

Rely upon solitude and powerful effort
And swiftly accomplish your eternal goal, my child!

THE IMPORTANCE OF COMPASSION

There are many different kinds of Dharma practice—hundreds of different mantras to recite, all kinds of meditation—but the most important of them all is the practice of compassion. Since each of us has taken personal responsibility for the happiness of each and every sentient being, our development of compassion becomes even more crucial.

If the practice of compassion, the good heart, is missing from your life, then no matter what other practices you do—even the profound, esoteric ones from the highest yoga tantra division of Mahayana secret mantra, which is undertaken for the express purpose of attaining buddhahood as quickly as possible for the sake of all sentient beings—they don't become the quick path to enlightenment that they're supposed to be. Without compassion, no practice can lead to enlightenment and can even become a cause of not only samsara in general but rebirth in the lower realms—the hell, hungry ghost or animal realms. Therefore, no matter how profound or advanced a practice might be considered—*dzog-chen,* the natural great perfection, or *dzog-rim,* the completion stage of highest yoga tantra—if it's done without the good heart, the intention of benefiting others, instead of being of benefit, it can be of harm. This is not the fault of the practice but of the practitioner who does it with improper motivation, with the wrong attitude.

If the practices you do—prayers, mantra recitation, meditation—are motivated by compassion towards all sentient beings, they become an incredibly skillful means of collecting vast amounts of merit and purifying the mind of eons of obscurations and negative karma.

This applies not only to formal practice. If everything you do in the course of a twenty-four hour day—walking, sitting, sleeping, working, talking, eating, whatever—is done with the good heart, with an attitude of compassion towards all sentient beings, then even if you don't have much time to do sitting meditation or other formal practices, all these regular daily activities are transformed into service for other sentient beings. Even if your life is fully occupied by work and family obligations, if you bring the essential practice, compassion, the thought of benefiting others, into everything you do, it becomes the best kind of Dharma, the cause of happiness and success for yourself and, more importantly, all the numberless other sentient beings.

Therefore, no matter how you lead your daily life—in retreat, studying Dharma, chanting sadhanas, reciting mantras or putting in long hours at the office—if you never let compassion leave your mind, if you constantly keep in mind the thought of benefiting others, everything you do becomes work for the welfare of others. Before, when what you did was motivated by ego and attachment, it was work for simply your own happiness. Therefore, everything you did was non-virtuous and created only negative karma, the cause of suffering. But now, like iron transformed into gold, the alchemy of compassion transforms your previously samsaric actions into the cause of not only happiness, peace and enlightenment for yourself, but also happiness for each and every sentient being without exception. Your life itself becomes like gold—pure, rich, extremely meaningful and highly beneficial. Your mind becomes a wealth of merit and good karma, the cause of every happiness.

If you keep the intention to benefit others in mind, if there's compassion for all sentient beings in your heart, even if you are just going to work, every step, every moment in your car, generates infinite merit in your mental continuum. Because your main goal is the happiness of all sentient beings, every step is very important, extremely precious. Every step you take creates merit as infinite as space.

If you are giving a speech with bodhicitta motivation, compassion, the thought of benefiting other sentient beings, every word, every sentence generates great good karma, the cause of happiness. Why? Because your speech is motivated by the wish for all sentient beings to experience happiness and benefit.

Similarly, if you eat and drink with the motivation of compassion for all sentient beings, every mouthful you swallow creates merit as vast as space. You collect infinite good karma, the cause of happiness. If you work at your job keeping the happiness and welfare of all sentient beings in your heart, every second, every minute, every hour you spend at work continuously generates infinite merit, boundless good karma, the cause of happiness in your mind. Every action that you do with bodhicitta motivation, compassion, the thought of benefiting others, becomes the cause of happiness of all sentient beings.

BODHICITTA TRANSFORMS YOUR LIFE

That's why Khedrup Rinpoche, one of Lama Tsong Khapa's two main disciples, wrote in his praise of his guru's good qualities, "Every breath you take is of benefit to all sentient beings." He said this because Lama Tsong Khapa had realized bodhicitta—renouncing himself and cherishing only others. If you have realized bodhicitta—the altruistic mind determined to achieve enlightenment for the sake of sentient beings, the thought of working only for the benefit of others—every single action of your body, speech and mind is dedicated to the welfare of others. Your entire life is lived completely for the sake of others. There's not even a second's thought for yourself, for your own happiness. Everything you do is solely for the happiness of other sentient beings. If you recite one rosary of mantras, it is done only for others; if you eat one bowl of food, it is only for others; if you drink one cup of tea, it is only for others. Every single thing you do is done only for others. Nothing in your life is not done for others, for their benefit.

The realization of bodhicitta, compassion, loving kindness, completely transforms your mind. With your old mind, you thought only of your own happiness and worked solely for the sake of self, your old self. The continuity of that mind has no beginning. Because of that mind, you're still mired in suffering, not free from samsara, and of extremely limited benefit to others. Since you have not developed your mind, your ability to work perfectly for other sentient beings, to bring them all happiness, including enlightenment, is very limited. The realization of bodhicitta turns all that upside down. It brings you a fresh attitude, a new mind—the kind of mind that Khedrup Rinpoche was talking about when he said of Lama Tsong Khapa, "Every time you breathe in or out, it brings happiness to all sentient beings."

There's a related story concerning the great enlightened being, Pabongka Rinpoche (1871–1941), a great lama, scholar and yogi who had actualized the entire path to enlightenment. He wrote not only lam-rim texts like *Liberation in the Palm of Your Hand* but also many other sutra scriptures and, especially, several excellent, extremely lucid commentaries on the tantras—really clear explanations of deity practices from his own experience. Of course, his writings were based on the teachings of Guru Shakyamuni Buddha and the commentaries of the ancient Indian and Tibetan pundits and yogis, but by practicing these he had his own experiences and actualized the entire path himself. Thus, he was able to write with great clarity on tantra and benefit the Dharma and all sentient beings in general. He had thousands of disciples, many of whom, on the basis of his teachings and guidance, had realizations of the three principal aspects of the path to enlightenment and, in particular, the path of secret mantra, the Vajrayana.

One of Pabongka Dechen Nyingpo's disciples was a lama called Togten Rinpoche. He had formerly been a practitioner of the Nyingma tradition—there are four main Tibetan Buddhist schools: Nyingma, Kagyu, Sakya and Gelug—but one day he came to discuss emptiness with a high Gelugpa lama called Denma Locho Rinpoche, whose present incarnation is one of my gurus. So Denma Locho Rinpoche advised Togten Rinpoche, "If you want to realize emptiness, you should go to Lhasa and meet Pabongka Rinpoche." So he went to Lhasa and received many teachings from Pabongka Dechen Nyingpo and practiced meditation under his guidance. Pabongka Rinpoche's monastery is not far from Sera Monastery, and high on the cliff above is his cave-hermitage, where Togten Rinpoche did his retreat.

He would practice his meditation, and whenever he had a realization, would come down to offer it to his guru, Pabongka Dechen Nyingpo. One day he attained the ninth level of meditative stabilization, the final step in the process of developing calm abiding. This is a very important realization because you have overcome both gross and subtle scattering and gross and subtle sinking, the main hindrances to perfect single-pointed concentration. It is a similitude of calm abiding, not the actual one, but it leads right into actual calm abiding. Togten Rinpoche must have been pretty excited at having attained this level of meditation, so he came down to tell his guru all about it. Now, before I get to the punch line of this story, I should give you an idea of exactly what Togten Rinpoche had accomplished.

THE FIVE PATHS

When you realize calm abiding, you can concentrate single-pointedly on whatever object you choose for as many months or years—even eons—as you like, as determined by your motivation. No matter how many distractions surround you—police sirens, train whistles, people beating drums in your ear—nothing can disturb your mind or interfere with your concentration. However long you plan to concentrate, that's how long you can keep your mind on the object, immovable as a mountain. Not only that, but you also experience rapturous ecstasy of body and mind. Your body feels as light as cotton, as if it could float away, and very, very healthy. You can use your body in any virtuous action or practice with no hardship or difficulty whatsoever. Your mind is so controlled that, as I mentioned, you can concentrate on any object for as long as you like, and if you let go of your mind, it automatically gravitates to virtuous objects—so there's no danger of creating any negative karma. The great advantage of having achieved calm abiding, however, is that it now becomes very easy for you to achieve other realizations. In particular, you can meditate on emptiness as your object in order to develop special insight and the wisdom that is the actual antidote to the suffering of samsara.

The Four Noble Truths, the foundation of Guru Shakyamuni

Buddha's teachings, are true suffering, true cause of suffering, true cessation of suffering and true path. True path means the wisdom directly perceiving emptiness, the very nature of phenomena, ultimate nature. This is what actually ceases the delusions—the cause of all suffering; the cause of the cycle of rebirth, aging, sickness and death; the cause of the hell realms, the hungry ghost realms, the animal realms and all the suffering those rebirths entail; and the cause of the human, asura and sura realms and all their suffering as well.

When you achieve the wisdom directly perceiving emptiness, you attain what's called the right-seeing path. It is here that the delusions, the obscurations, the defilements, actually begin to cease. In all, there are five paths to liberation from suffering and its cause—the paths of merit, preparation (or conjunction), right-seeing, meditation and no more learning. By developing the wisdom realizing emptiness motivated by the method of renunciation of samsara—the determination to free yourself from samsara—you can achieve your own liberation. By achieving the right-seeing path, you remove 112 disturbing thought obscurations, and on the path of meditation, 16 disturbing thought obscurations.

However, you destroy not only the delusions, but their seed as well, so that it becomes no longer possible for them ever to arise again. That means you will never again create karma or have to experience suffering. You become an *arhant,* your holy mind free from the obscurations of the disturbing thoughts. You attain nirvana, the sorrowless state, and liberate yourself from the entire round of samsaric suffering.

To achieve enlightenment for the benefit of numberless other sentient beings, you need to achieve the five Mahayana paths, which are also called merit, preparation, right-seeing, meditation and no more learning. Here, no more learning means omniscient mind, the completion of all understanding; there's not a single object of knowledge left to discover. Again, it is on the Mahayana right-seeing path that your wisdom directly perceiving emptiness starts ceasing the delusions. Anyway, there are many details of these paths and many texts describing them, of which the *Abhisamayalamkara* is probably the best known. In the great Tibetan monasteries, such as Sera, Ganden and Drepung, the monks study many root texts and commentaries that detail the five paths and so forth. They memorize, debate and meditate for thirty or forty years. It's a bit like one person trying to learn all the parts of an airplane and how they function together so that it can fly safely.

Anyway, to attain your own liberation from samsara, you need to understand the details of the five paths. The right-seeing path eliminates intellectual wrong conceptions, those acquired from incorrect teachings, while the path of meditation eradicates the innate misconceptions, the ones you were born with and have had in your mental continuum since beginningless time. After that, you reach the fifth path, that of no more learning, and attain nirvana, the sorrowless state.

To reach enlightenment for the sake of all sentient beings, you have to follow the five Mahayana paths. When you achieve the Mahayana right-seeing path, you also eradicate the gross obscurations (*nyön-drib*, in Tibetan), which prevent you from attaining your own liberation from samsara, but in addition, you eradicate the subtle obscurations (*she-drib*), the negative imprints left on your mental continuum by the gross delusions, which prevent you from attaining enlightenment.

MERELY LABELED

We believe that there's an I, a real self, in our body. But if you look for it, if you analyze the appearance to see whether or not the I really exists in your body, or on your aggregates, you can't find it. If you don't analyze, it looks like it's there, but if you do, you discover that it's non-existent. This is what your wisdom discovers. When you do not analyze, do not meditate, when you haven't realized the ultimate nature—the emptiness of the I, the ultimate nature of the self—it appears as if there's a real I there, in your body or on your five aggregates of body and mind. When you search with wisdom, you discover that the real I, appearing from there, is totally non-existent. It exists nowhere. That absence of the real I is what we call emptiness, or *shunyata,* the very nature of the self. That is the reality of the self. That's what the I is. It is empty—empty of the real I that appears from there—and exists merely in name. The only reason the I exists at all is because of the existence of a valid base, the aggregates. The five aggregates—form, feeling, cognition, compounding aggregates and consciousness—are a valid base for labeling "I," therefore the I exists.

For example, a child is born and its parents give it a name, a label. First the child, an association of body and mind, is actualized; then comes the label. So, depending on the base, let's say the parents call the child Richard. First the base comes into existence, then the label is applied. The base is not one with the label, "Richard." If it were, as soon as the base came into being, so would the label, "Richard." But the two are different. The child—the association of body and mind, the aggregates—and the label—the name, "Richard"—are not separate, but they're different. Similarly, our base—the association of our body and mind, our aggregates—is not one with the label "I." The base and the label do not exist separately, but they exist differently. The definition of why Richard exists is because the association of body and mind—the base that can receive the label "Richard"— exists. Richard exists because his base exists. That's the main reason. Similarly, the only reason the I exists is because the base, the association of body and mind, exists—the valid base that *can* receive the label "I." Because of that, the self exists.

But our deluded minds do not see this. To us it appears as if the I exists from the side of the aggregates, as if there's a real self there. But by analyzing this appearance and your belief in it, you can discover that what you see and believe is a hallucination. The real I that appears from there is completely non-existent. There's not an atom of real self there. In reality, it is non-existent, but not recognizing this, not realizing this, believing the illusion to be real, believing one hundred percent that the I that appears from there is its reality, blocks you from seeing the ultimate, empty nature of the I.

The I that exists, that experiences happiness and suffering, that walks, talks, eats, sits and sleeps is nothing other than what has been merely labeled by the mind. But even though that merely labeled I exists, if you look for it on the aggregates, on the base, you cannot find it anywhere, from the ends of your hair to the tips of your toes. There's no question that the merely labeled I exists. It's just that you can't find it on the base, on your aggregates.

The I that appears to you in your body or on your aggregates as not merely labeled by the mind—as if it has nothing to do with your mind, as if there's a real I there that never came from your mind, that exists from its own side—is the I that does not exist. Neither in your body nor on your aggregates nor anywhere else—that I exists nowhere. This is reality. The absence of such an I, the emptiness of that, is the ultimate nature of the I.

The hallucinating mind—the wrong conception holding on to the I as not merely labeled by the mind, as existing from its own side; holding as true that something real is appearing from there—is the root of all delusion, karma and suffering. This unknowing mind, this ignorance, is the main suffering. This hallucinating mind—the wrong conception that believes the I to be other than it really is, in completely the wrong way—is our worst suffering. This is the basic ignorance that we have to eradicate in order to escape from all suffering and its cause.

The only way to do this is to realize emptiness. The wisdom realizing the emptiness of the I is the only solution, the only direct remedy, for this wrong conception. By developing this wisdom we can remove all delusions, liberate ourselves from suffering, and, by revealing the truth to others, liberate numberless other sentient beings as well.

MORE ABOUT THE FIVE PATHS

Before going off on that tangent of emptiness, I was explaining the five paths. There are five paths to nirvana—individual liberation from samsara—and five Mahayana paths to enlightenment. To complete these paths, first you have to achieve calm abiding (*shamatha*), by proceeding through the nine levels of meditative stabilization. Then you have to realize special insight (*vipashyana*), and finally achieve the wisdom realizing emptiness, the great concentration—the wisdom realizing emptiness unified with calm abiding.

If your motivation is not bodhicitta but simply renunciation of samsara, at that point you achieve the path of preparation, which is the basis for achieving the right-seeing path, the true path of the Four Noble Truths. At that level, as I mentioned above, the intellectual wrong conceptions are eliminated, and on the fourth path, the path of meditation—as the wisdom directly perceiving emptiness is further developed—the innate defilements are eradicated.

Following the Mahayana, on the basis of having achieved bodhicitta—the compassionate loving thought, the altruistic mind set on achieving enlightenment for sentient beings, renouncing yourself and cherishing others—and the wisdom realizing emptiness unified with calm abiding, you achieve the Mahayana path of preparation. That is the basis for achieving the Mahayana right-seeing path, the wisdom directly perceiving emptiness.

There are two ways of entering the Mahayana path. Either you can enter directly by first developing bodhicitta, or you can first complete the five Hinayana paths as either a solitary realizer or a hearer by becoming an arhant, and then enter the Mahayana in order to attain enlightenment. On the Mahayana right-seeing path, you remove 112 gross and 108 subtle obscurations, and on the path of meditation, 16 gross and 108 subtle. Then you achieve the Mahayana path of no more learning, full enlightenment.

INCOMPARABLE BODHICITTA

I have explained the above to give you an idea of how great an achievement it is to have progressed through the nine levels of meditative stabilization and to achieve calm abiding. Now to get back to the story.

When Togten Rinpoche arrived, extremely pleased that he had reached the ninth level of meditative stabilization, Pabongka Dechen Nyingpo was in the middle of eating a lunch of *pak*—a dense ball of *tsampa,* the Tibetan staple of roasted barley flour, mixed with tea and butter. But Togten Rinpoche couldn't wait, and reported his experience anyway. When he had finished, Pabongka replied, "Compared to the benefits of my eating this pak, your realization is nothing!"

Even though the attainment of calm abiding is incredible and has inconceivable benefits—rapturous ecstasy, unsurpassed clarity of mind, unshakable single-pointed concentration, freedom from sickness due to refinement of body and mind—it doesn't have bodhicitta: compassion, loving kindness, renouncing yourself and cherishing others. Pabongka, however, had realized bodhicitta. Therefore, every mouthful of pak he ate was work for all sentient beings without exception. Naturally, effortlessly, each mouthful of food created infinite merit, as limitless as the sky. This story, therefore, illustrates the benefits of bodhicitta and shows how practicing the good heart can make our lives most practical and beneficial.

When Lama Yeshe—who was kinder than the buddhas of the three times and took care of me like a father cherishes his only son, not only with education but also with food and clothing and all other means of living—was in Delhi on his way to America for treatment, there was a discussion about a student who had done something wrong, and Lama was asked if he was angry with him. "How could I possibly be angry with him?" Lama replied. "He's a sentient being." That shows that Lama had realized bodhicitta. If you don't have realization, just the knowledge that someone is a suffering sentient being isn't enough to prevent you from getting angry.

AWARENESS AND THE SELF

Student: May I ask a question, please? You were speaking before about the illusory nature of the I. What's the difference between that itself and the awareness of it?

Rinpoche: The awareness that recognizes things is mind. That awareness is not the I, the self. The mind is a part of the base. In this life you have a body and a mind. This association of body and mind is the base that you label I. Body and mind are the base; I is the label. The base and the label are two different phenomena. Not only that. I is the possessor; mind, that which is possessed. When you say "*My* mind," I is the possessor and mind is the possession. They are subject and object; two different things, not one. Therefore, the awareness that recognizes things is not I. It is neither the real I—the I that appears to us not merely labeled by the mind—nor even the merely labeled I. But just because you cannot find the I on your aggregates, from the tips of your hair down to your toes—the body is not I; the mind is not I; even the association of both is not I; the I cannot be found anywhere—does not mean that it does not exist. The I exists. The I, the self, cannot be found on your aggregates, the association of your body and mind. The real I that appears from there cannot be found. Even the merely labeled I cannot be found there. But that doesn't mean that the I does not exist in this room. It exists in this room; it exists in America. But it doesn't exist on your association of body and mind.

As long as your body and mind are in this room, the I cannot be found on that base, but it exists in this room. But the only reason for saying that it exists in this room and is not at home right now is that the association of your body and mind are in this room. That's the only reason. Even though you cannot find the I on them. The minute your body and mind leave the room, so does the I; it is no longer present in this room. So, what is that I? It is nothing other than what has been merely imputed by the mind because of the existence of the base, the association of body and mind.

By analyzing your I in this way, you can come to see that it is totally something else, completely different from what you've always thought it was, from beginningless rebirths up to the present. All this time your mind has merely been labeling I on the association of body and mind, and that is how it exists. But every time your mind has merely labeled I, it doesn't appear back to you as if it's been merely labeled. That's the problem. If the I did always appear to you as merely labeled by the mind, it would be impossible for you to generate anger, jealousy, grasping, attachment and all the other painful emotional minds. If you were able to perceive the I as merely labeled by the mind there would be no base upon which delusions could arise. Then you wouldn't create motivating karma, suffering or samsara itself.

What happens is that after your mind merely labels I, when it appears back to you it does not appear as if it has been merely labeled by the mind. It appears back in completely the opposite way, as if it has *not* been merely labeled by the mind. That is the hallucination.

Therefore, the reality of the I that is merely labeled by the mind is that it is totally empty. It exists, but it is totally empty. It exists, but it is totally empty of existing from its own side. While it is empty of existing from its own side, the I exists. How? In mere name. When you realize this, you have gained an unmistaken realization of empti-ness. On the single object, I, you are able to unify dependent arising and emptiness. The I itself is both empty yet existent. It exists, but it is empty. When you realize these two, without division, you have gained an unmistaken realization of emptiness. If, in what you think is a realization of emptiness, you cannot unify these two or find a contradiction with existence, then your so-called realization of emptiness is wrong. When it comes to this point and you cannot define how the I exists, you cannot see the existence of the I, that means your realization of emptiness is not the actual realization of emptiness but just ordinary emptiness.

When you analyze, the I becomes extremely subtle—so subtle that even though it is not non-existent, it is as if it were non-existent. It is not non-existent, but it seems to be non-existent. It appears not to exist; it becomes an unbelievably subtle phenomenon. The line of demarcation between the existence and the non-existence of the I is extremely fine, extremely subtle. So fine that what is existent appears to be almost non-existent. What it is, however, is merely labeled by the mind.

PATIENCE AND THE COMPASSIONATE HEART

Guru Shakyamuni Buddha said,

> Do not engage in any harmful actions;
> Perform only those that are good;
> Subdue your own mind—
> This is the teaching of the Buddha.

What did he mean? The above verse encapsulates the entire teaching of the kind, compassionate Buddha. In it, he is telling us sentient beings, who want only happiness and do not want suffering, how to achieve our aims.

Where do happiness and suffering come from?

Happiness and suffering do not come from outside but from actions motivated by our own minds, our own thoughts. Happiness comes from positive actions. Problems come from mistaken, or unskillful, actions. Positive actions, pure actions, are motivated by a positive, virtuous attitude, the pure mind, the healthy mind, the peaceful mind.

All happiness—the transient happiness of our everyday lives, and ultimate happiness, both liberation and enlightenment—comes from each being's positive attitude and virtuous actions; from the pure mind. Liberation is the complete cessation of all suffering, including rebirth, aging, sickness and death, and its cause. Enlightenment, the great liberation, which is even higher than this, is the cessation of even the subtle defilements of mind and the completion of all realizations. Each and every sentient being has the potential to experience all this. It comes from positive motivation and good karma. All suffering comes from each being's negative attitude and non-virtuous actions.

In your life, until your mind labels something as a problem, before you have the concept of problem, you don't have any problems. Before your mind fabricates the label, "problem," you don't see problems in your life. What do I mean by concept here? It's where your thought interprets a certain situation as a problem. In other words, your mind creates the designation "problem" for this particular situation. Before that happens, you don't see any problem with the situation, but the moment your mind creates the label, "problem," and believes in it, that is the moment that the concept of problem has been created. You have created the concept of life problem.

This is just a simple example of how problems come from your own mind, how problems depend upon your own concepts, how problems depend upon the very concept of problem. The problems in your life depend upon your having the concept of problem—having the thought, creating the label and believing in it. This is just a very simple example of how your problems depend upon your own mind. It shows how your problems depend upon the thought, or concept, you have at that moment—that hour, that minute, that second—how this hour's problem, this minute's problem is related to, or comes from, the way you are thinking at the time. The present moment's problem comes from the present moment's thought, or concept, which creates the label and believes in it.

Anger is another example of this. If you don't create the mental factor, or thought, of anger, there are no enemies in your life; you can't find any enemies. If you don't form the thought of anger, wherever you go, wherever in the world you travel, wherever you live, whoever you're with, you never see a single enemy. If you don't create anger within, you have no enemy outside.

DON'T BE YOURSELF

If you do not practice compassion, loving kindness and patience towards others, if you do not cultivate these healthy minds, these positive, beneficial thoughts for the sake of yourself and all other sentient beings, if you don't make an effort to develop these positive attitudes, you are just being yourself; you are allowing yourself to be your old self. Your old self follows your ego and self-centered mind and thinks only of your own happiness and nothing else. From beginningless time, in every rebirth, your old self has been under the influence of ego and self-centeredness, the unhealthy, uptight, unpeaceful mind. Your old self's heart is closed, not open. Your old self works only for your own happiness and cares nothing for the needs of others. Your old self does not think that you are responsible for the happiness of others, that your happiness comes from others and that their happiness depends upon you. Your old, self-centered mind thinks only of your own happiness and nothing other than that.

So "being yourself" means just this—being your old self. Instead of practicing those positive minds, you do just the opposite. You follow disturbing thoughts such as attachment and anger, which offer your mind no peace, no rest, no realization—only agitation, trouble and unhappiness. There's no holiday for your mind. Even if you take your body on vacation, there's no vacation for your mind, no rest and relaxation for your mental continuum. The result of continually following your old self—ego, attachment and anger—is that you never find satisfaction. These thoughts can never bring you satisfaction, no matter for how many eons you follow them. This is simply the nature of attachment.

As Guru Shakyamuni Buddha said, "As long as you follow desire you will never be satisfied." It's like sitting in a fire. As long as you sit in a fire you will never experience the pleasure of not being burned. If you long to be comfortable and cool, you have to get out. In just the same way, as that is logical, so is it logical that as long as you follow attachment you will not find inner peace, true satisfaction, real rest. There's no vacation for your heart. That's the old self at work. When the Rolling Stones sang, "Well, I tried and I tried, I tried and I tried—I can't get no, satisfaction," they were actually giving a lam-rim teaching; a lam-rim teaching with guitar accompaniment. They were teaching meditation.

If you don't have a good heart, if you have no satisfaction—which can be experienced only by not following the painful minds of desire and attachment—if you don't develop loving kindness and compassion, then even if you do take a break from your job and take your body to the beach, there's no rest for your mind. There's no peace within your mental continuum because you have taken with you your attachment and anger and the constant problems they create. Because you lack a good heart and cannot dedicate yourself to others, there's no fulfillment in your heart. Because of the disturbing emotional thoughts of attachment and anger, you get no satisfaction and experience constant problems.

Your emotional thoughts are the foundation of all problems. They themselves are the main problem. Because of them, you have no inner peace and cannot enjoy your life. Even though externally it might look as if you're enjoying yourself, as if you're experiencing excitement and pleasure, when you look into your heart, you know that there's always something missing. Only by giving up— cutting, freeing yourself from—disturbing emotional thoughts, such as the painful mind of attachment, can you find satisfaction in your heart, in your inner life.

If you can stop being your old self, if you can stop following the beginningless discriminating thoughts of attachment and anger, stop forming the thought of anger, stop transforming the mind that was not angry into one that wants to harm others, you will never have enemies. Wherever you go, you will never find an enemy trying to harm you.

ELIMINATING ENEMIES

What do you do when you encounter someone who doesn't love you, who's angry at you? You practice patience. Instead of interpreting that person's actions as *negative,* or *harmful,* you interpret them as *positive,* or *beneficial.* Instead of thinking how harmful it is that the person is angry at you, doesn't love you, think how beneficial, how necessary, how useful it is. Just as you feel it important to have in your life someone who loves you, feel it just as necessary to have someone who doesn't love you. Think how much you need the person who is angry at you. Feel that the person who dislikes you is just as precious as the one who has compassion for you. Instead of seeing it as negative, see it as positive, beneficial.

If right at that moment, instead of telling yourself how harmful it is, you practice patience by thinking how useful it is, if instead of thinking how useless it is, you think how necessary it is, you will immediately experience peace and tranquillity in your mind. Instead of being troubled, you'll be happy, then and there. Moreover, you won't be impelled to retaliate and will therefore refrain from harming others. In this way you will avoid creating the negative karma of injuring others with body, speech and mind.

If out of anger you give harm to others, you leave negative imprints on your own mental continuum. These then manifest as problems in this life, future lives or both—problems such as sickness, ill-treatment at the hands of others, premature death and so forth. These are called "karmic results similar to the cause in experience," and we create them ourselves by responding negatively to those who are angry at us.

Therefore, by practicing patience, you don't harm others and thus don't harm yourself. If you don't practice patience, you do harm others and therefore harm yourself. Furthermore, when you practice patience and refrain from harming others, you protect them from retaliating in response to your harm, thereby saving them from creating extra negative karma, the cause of suffering—you protect others from having to experience the karmic results of giving you harm. Thus, by practicing patience, besides creating the cause of happiness for yourself in this and future lives, you help others to experience happiness in this and future lives.

As a result of your practicing patience and not harming the person who's angry at you, that other person doesn't give you further harm.

Not only is there peace and happiness for yourself and the other person in this and future lives, but you are also training your mind to be patient with others. This person is helping you do that. You are learning to be patient with the rest of your family, the rest of your colleagues, all other human beings and all sentient beings in general. The person who is angry with you is helping you train your mind to be patient and positive instead of angry and negative.

As you eradicate anger from your mental continuum and replace it with patience, the rest of the sentient beings receive no harm from you, the individual whose mind has been transformed into patience. The absence of harm, their not receiving harm from you, is peace. What they receive from you is happiness.

THE BENEFITS OF PATIENCE

Historically, you can see how, at different times and in different places in the world, one influential person who did not practice patience caused millions of people to die. As a result, many millions of people underwent extraordinary suffering by being imprisoned, tortured and killed—during the Hitler era, in China, in Tibet, in Cambodia, in the West and in many other countries as well. Even now, because they do not practice patience, certain individuals are killing many people. They lack the qualities that make a person good.

Now, consider yourself in light of the above. As an individual practicing patience, learning to be patient, by freeing your mind of anger, you can offer great peace and happiness to numberless other sentient beings, not only in this life, but in many future lives to come. Since there's no anger, you don't harm others. Therefore, many people, animals, fish and insects, for example, receive much peace and happiness from you. Thus, life to life, with patience towards all sentient beings, you bring significant peace and happiness to the world. By practicing patience you give peace to the world—to your parents, the rest of your family, your friends, the people you work with and, on the grand scale, all sentient beings.

Leaving aside other realizations of the path, if those powerful people had only been educated in, possessed and practiced the good human quality of patience, the good heart, each could have given so much happiness to the world. Many millions of people would have had happiness, enjoyment and long lives instead of just the opposite. One person could have made so much difference had he only been patient instead of angry. Put yourself into this situation. This could happen to you. If you don't practice patience in this or future lives, you, too, could be reborn as someone who harms millions of people. Therefore, you definitely need to practice patience. You should consider it a responsibility. It is extremely important that you educate yourself in patience and practice it. It is perhaps the most important meditation you can do.

If you practice patience, you eliminate anger. That means there's no enemy to bodhicitta in your mind. In other words, it makes it much easier to achieve bodhicitta, the ultimate good heart, the altruistic mind set on attaining enlightenment for the sake of all sentient beings. Bodhicitta is the gateway to the Mahayana path, the root of the path to enlightenment and the source of all happiness for both yourself and others.

By actualizing the perfection of patience, you can attain full enlightenment, the great liberation, the cessation of all mental errors and the completion of all realizations. Once you have attained enlightenment, you are free to work perfectly for the welfare of all sentient beings in order to liberate them from all suffering and its cause and bring them to buddhahood as well. This is the long term benefit of practicing patience in your daily life right now, a benefit as measureless as space itself.

Practicing patience today will allow you to become the perfect guide and bring all happiness to numberless sentient beings. Therefore, when somebody treats you badly or when someone gets angry at you, these are the benefits of not getting upset. You can look at it differently. You can see how responding with patience is the source of all happiness—not only your own immediate happiness but also that of your future lives; not only your own happiness, but that of number-less others. You can make it all happen. It comes from your patience.

Patience has many other benefits as well. For example, practicing patience is the cause of receiving a beautiful body in future lives—a beautiful human body or the divine body of a *deva*. If your body is attractive, it is easier to benefit others. It is also the cause of many of the special qualities of a buddha's holy body. There are many more benefits of patience.

If you do not practice patience, you will get angry. One of the results of anger is to receive ugly bodies in future lives. If you look ugly, people won't want to see or hear you, won't want to help you and won't pay attention to what you say. Worse than that, you will have to experience the unbearably heavy sufferings of rebirth in hell. And even when, after that, you're reborn human, there will be many other problems as a result of anger. Anger has many, many drawbacks, but by practicing patience you can avoid them all.

In short, practicing patience on a daily basis has infinite benefit. It brings peace, happiness and success for yourself and others in this and many future lives. Ultimately, you attain enlightenment, and bring all happiness to all sentient beings as you lead them to enlightenment.

HOW TO PRACTICE PATIENCE

Where does your daily practice of patience that brings all this benefit come from? How did you learn to be patient?

Ask yourself, "Where did I learn this patience that I practice? I learned it from those who have been angry at me. By depending on the angry person I have been able to practice, to realize patience. Therefore, all the peace and happiness that I enjoy in this and future lives as a result of my practice of patience has come from the angry person. It is through the kindness of the angry person, who gave me the opportunity to practice patience, that I am able to offer peace and happiness to all sentient beings as a result. Because of this person I am able to accomplish the perfection of patience, the other perfections, and thereby complete the bodhisattva's path and attain full enlightenment. Through this person's kindness I can eradicate all errors of mind and gain all realizations. It is the angry person who has given me this opportunity. This person is actually giving me enlightenment. Through the kindness of this person I can also offer all peace and happiness to all sentient beings. How kind this person is! How much benefit this person has given me! This is the most precious person in my life! Even if someone were to give me billions and trillions of dollars, I could never buy the peace of mind that I get through the practice of patience. Therefore, the angry person who gives me the opportunity to practice patience is of much greater value than trillions of dollars, mountains of diamonds, acres of gold."

The angry person is even more precious than trillions of wish-fulfilling jewels. The most precious material object we can think of in these examples is the wish-fulfilling jewel. Legend has it that by praying to this mythical gem, you get whatever sense enjoyment you desire. Nevertheless, the angry person with whom you practice patience is far more valuable than trillions of these wish-granting gems. No amount of material wealth can bring you the inner peace that you can achieve by practicing patience with an angry person. That's why such people are so precious.

The only reason the person is so kind and precious is because he is angry at you. There's no reason other than that. This is what makes this person so unbelievably kind. Therefore, even though his anger is so destructive for him, for you it is invaluable. It is of the utmost need in your life. Having somebody angry at you is very, very important.

Say there were a cure for cancer or AIDS. We would regard that medicine as incredibly precious, extremely important, especially if we were suffering from one of those diseases. But even though such remedies could cure those fatal illnesses, it doesn't mean that they could purify your negative karma. They couldn't stop you from being reborn in the suffering lower realms—the hell, hungry ghost or animal realms. Practicing patience, however, does offer that kind of benefit. For example, the practice of patience makes for a happy, peaceful death, a death free from fear and worry. Practicing patience purifies, or counteracts, negative karma. When you practice patience, you don't create negative karma. That means you are not creating the cause for a lower rebirth—patience protects you from that. In fact, the practice of patience creates only positive karma, the cause of good rebirths.

Anyway, in order to practice patience, you need an angry person. As the great bodhisattva Shantideva pointed out in his teaching, the *Bodhicharyavatara,* the Buddha isn't angry with you, so you can't practice patience with him. And a doctor's only thought is to help you, so there's no opportunity there either. Similarly, your friends aren't angry with you, so there's no chance to practice patience with them. Therefore, if there's nobody angry at you, there's no opportunity to put into practice the teachings you've received from the Buddha and your gurus. That's why the angry person is most kind, precious and indispensable in your life, and much more important than medicine for cancer or AIDS. We think those medicines are so valuable, but when you think about it this way, you can see how much more precious the angry person is. The benefits of practicing patience are infinite.

We always want in our life someone who loves us. We feel that this is important for our happiness. But you can see now that it's much more important to have in our life someone who doesn't love us, who's angry at us, so that we can practice training our minds. As I mentioned before, if you don't have such a person, if you don't train your mind, then even if you do find a friend, there's the danger that through lack of patience, you'll turn your friend into an enemy.

Therefore, to maintain harmonious relationships with others, to keep your friends, you have to practice patience. To lead a happy and successful life, you almost have to train yourself like a soldier preparing for battle. Soldiers train before marching off to war. You need to do the same. Training your mind by practicing meditation on patience is the way to prepare yourself for the battles of daily life. Leaving aside the happiness of future lives or that of other sentient beings, even for the happiness of this life, you have to practice patience.

THE POWER OF POSITIVE THINKING

So now, going back to what I was saying before, look at the indescrib-able benefits of seeing in a positive light those who don't love you, those who are angry at you. Look at the profits you can reap—every happiness all the way up to enlightenment and the ability to bring every happiness to all sentient beings. The more clearly you under-stand this, the easier it will be to look positively at someone who is angry with you. In this way, your own anger does not arise and you generate a happy, peaceful, patient mind instead.

No matter how angry at you the other person gets, no matter how much the other person whines and complains, your patient mind never sees that person as an enemy, as someone to avoid, as someone to get away from, as irritating. Rather, you see that person as kind, precious. You feel, "She's purifying my negative karma. All this criti-cism of me helps purify my negative karma of having criticized and harmed others. How kind she is to help me in this way."

By transforming your mind into patience like this, you get this immediate peace and happiness—that day, that minute, that second—and the long-term benefits as well. All this is due to the kindness of that angry person. If you do not practice patience, if you interpret what the angry person is doing with her body, speech and mind as negative, as harmful to yourself—your mind applies a nega-tive label to the situation and you believe in that—your own anger will arise. That anger will make you see the angry person as negative, undesirable, someone you want to neither see nor help, someone you want to lash out at and hurt. When your mind is angry you see the other person in a completely different light, opposite to the way in which your patience perceives that person. Your anger makes her look repulsive.

The happiness and difficulties we experience every day come from our minds. Whatever we're experiencing at any given moment is dependent upon the way we think, our concepts, our attitude. Our attitude determines how we feel.

For example, once in Tibet there were a couple of monks who returned to their monastery after a long and tiring journey. To welcome them back, their teacher offered them cold tea. One of the disciples thought, "How kind our teacher is. He knew we were hot and thirsty so he intentionally gave us tea that was cold." The other thought, "How mean and lazy. He couldn't even give us hot tea," and got upset and angry. So, he destroyed himself. There was no benefit from the way he thought to either himself or his teacher. But, by having a positive view, the first student made himself and his teacher happy, made his mind peaceful and, since the tea had been offered by his guru, created much merit. The action—offering cold tea—was the same. What was different were the students' interpretations of that action. One labeled it positive and was happy. The other labeled it negative and created a problem for himself.

I started this talk with a quotation from Guru Shakyamuni Buddha:

Do not engage in any harmful actions;
Perform only those that are good;
Subdue your own mind—
This is the teaching of the Buddha.

The first line refers to the cause of suffering, the second the cause of happiness. The discussion of the importance and benefits of patience evolved from that. Everything comes from your mind, everything depends upon the way you think, your moment to moment concepts. Do you label things negatively or positively? The heaviest suffering, what we call hell, comes from your own mind; the greatest happiness, what we call enlightenment, comes from your own mind.

Therefore, the Buddha is saying that the way to never have negative thoughts, the cause of suffering, and to have only a positive mind, which results in only happiness, is to subdue, or take care of, your own mind. Watch your mind all the time. Practice mindfulness. Guard your mind, protect it from disturbing thoughts and eradicate your delusions. How is all that done? Through actualizing the five paths. In the case of the Mahayana, by actualizing bodhicitta and developing the wisdom realizing emptiness. Through the wisdom directly perceiving emptiness, you can completely remove the two types of defilement and attain full enlightenment.

Therefore, subduing the mind is the teaching of the Buddha. That's the key. Your own mind is the door to happiness; your own mind is the door to suffering. It all depends upon how you use it. It's like the remote control that controls the channels on your TV. Click it this way, it goes up; click it that way, it goes down. The way you think determines whether you'll experience happiness or suffering.

WHAT CREATES THE LABELS?

Before I finish, I'll make one more point. Like the monks in the story above, our minds are constantly making up labels that affect our lives. Depending upon the label, we experience different feelings—pleasant, unpleasant or neutral—and that's how our life goes, twenty-four hours a day. So, what is it that causes our minds to create these different labels? People who apply positive labels experience happiness. People who apply negative labels experience suffering. What is it, then, that causes us to label things positive or negative? What's the force behind all this?

It's karma. Because of past karma, some people are able to label things positively while others have to label them negatively. The underlying cause is karma. Therefore, you can see how crucial it is to purify past negative karma and not to create any more—in other words, how essential it is to practice Dharma. Only the practice of Dharma can remove or prevent the negative karma that forces us to label things negatively, thereby creating our own suffering. Dharma is the solution to all life's problems, whatever they are, and, more importantly, the sole means of preventing them from arising in the first place.

By practicing Dharma now we can avoid creating the causes for the heaviest sufferings of samsara, those of the lower realms—the hell, hungry ghost and animal realms—and the sufferings we go through in the upper realms, even as humans—illnesses such as cancer and AIDS, aging, death, everything—and thus avoid having to experience them. By practicing Dharma now we can purify the already created karma of such results. Here is where the whole answer to our problems lies—purify the negative karma already created; do not create any more. This is the reason we take precepts such as the refuge vow, the five lay precepts, not to mention the ordination vows taken by monks and nuns. You don't even have to take all five precepts. You can take one, two, three or four—whatever you can manage. Of course, there are countless negative karmas, but at least you can vow not to create certain kinds.

By practicing Dharma today we also create the causes for our own happiness—the happiness of this life, future lives, liberation and enlightenment. This is something we can do right now. Therefore, it is essential to create as much good karma as possible, while we have the chance. We should take every opportunity to create even the tiniest merit. Since we want even the smallest comfort, we have to create its cause. Similarly, since we don't want to experience even the smallest suffering or inconvenience, we have to avoid creating even the tiniest non-virtue. As it says in the Vinaya teaching, *Dulwa lung,* "Small drops fill a big pot." Therefore, we shouldn't think that small merits are useless. Try to collect as many as possible. It also says, "A tiny spark can ignite a huge forest." Therefore, don't think that small negative karmas won't bring results. Avoid them too. Here is where we must direct all our effort. This is the Buddha's fundamental advice.

MEDITATION ON EMPTINESS

Once again, bring your attention away from hallucination to the realities of life, the nature of which is impermanence and death. Awareness of death helps free our mind from delusion and karma so that we can not only bring to an end the entire round of suffering, the cycle of death and rebirth, but also eradicate even the subtle errors of mind, thereby attaining enlightenment for the sake of all sentient beings.

All causative phenomena—our life, our body, our mind, our self, our possessions, our relatives and friends, all other people—are changing, not only day by day, minute by minute and second by second, but every tiny moment. They do not last for a fraction of a second. Because they are under the control of causes and conditions, they are in a state of constant decay and can cease at any time. This is the nature of our life. If we can remain aware of this, we will prevent our mind from coming under the control of the delusions—the disturbing emotional minds that hurt us and other sentient beings, prevent us from transforming our mind and gaining realizations of the path to enlightenment, and stop us from seeing the ultimate nature of all phenomena. First we stop delusions from manifesting, and then, by actualizing the remedial path, we eradicate even the imprints that they have left on our mental continuum. By destroying the seeds of delusion, we attain nirvana, ultimate liberation from the six realms of suffering and its cause, freedom from the circling aggregates, which are samsara itself. These are the benefits of mindfulness of impermanence. We free ourselves of disturbing thoughts, immediately experience peace and satisfaction, free ourselves from samsara, and eventually attain enlightenment and enlighten all sentient beings.

Contemplate all this.

Now meditate on emptiness, the actual nature of all phenomena. Think how your I, actions, objects, and in fact all phenomena—everything that is called "such and such" and "this and that"—are just names. Names have to come from the mind; they don't exist from their own side. Names are labels applied by the mind. However, it is not just that phenomena are labeled by the mind—they are *merely* labeled by the mind. In other words, all phenomena—I, action, object, everything—are merely labeled by the mind, in relation to their base.

Think about this.

HOW THINGS EXIST

Now I'm going to elaborate a little on the subject of emptiness. The way in which everything exists is by being merely labeled by the mind. But that does not mean that everything the mind labels actually exists. Even though everything exists by being merely labeled by the mind, that doesn't mean that if your mind labels something it automatically brings it into existence.

For example, say I cut up a huge pile of newspapers into little pieces and my mind labels each one "a billion dollars"—that doesn't make each piece of paper worth a billion dollars. Even though my mind has merely labeled those pieces of paper "a billion dollars," that doesn't mean each one has become a billion dollars.

If it were possible for that to happen, we wouldn't have to vote in presidential elections. We wouldn't have to put all that effort into raising funds, campaigning, spending all that money, holding inquiries, to elect the president. All you'd have to do would be to label yourself, "I'm the American president," and you'd become president. If things coming into existence were only up to the mind labeling them, if that's all it took, then that's what would happen. Whenever you wanted to be president, all you'd have to do would be to have your mind label yourself president and you'd be president. In that way, everybody could become president. Maybe there'd be nobody left who wasn't president.

A magician could hypnotize you into believing that he'd given you a bag full of money, and you might carry it home, believing you were rich, but later, when you opened it up, there'd be nothing there but cut up pieces of newspaper. That's one way of showing that it doesn't exist—for your own mind to discover that it's not true. Later, when you're not under the influence of hypnosis, you realize that it was an illusion, that the money you saw didn't exist. Everything was there for your mind—the appearance of money and your mind labeling it money—but it wasn't money.

Another way of showing that it does not exist is for other people not to see the money. Because of the illusion created by hypnosis, money appears to your mind, but other people, whose minds are not under the illusion, don't see it. Therefore, it takes more than appearance and labeling by mind for something to exist.

Dreams are another example of something where your own mind can discover that appearance and labeling by mind are insufficient to bring something into existence. For instance, one night you might have a dream in which you became king, got married in a huge wedding ceremony, lived in a luxurious jeweled palace and had many children. While you are dreaming, the appearance of all this and your mind merely labeling it are both there, but when you wake up you again realize it wasn't true. You're not king, there's no palace, no wealth, no princes and princesses—nothing. You don't have any of that.

A VALID BASE

For things to exist, mere labeling by mind is not enough. There has to be a valid base. Not just any base—a valid base. Therefore, I cannot label my bell "car." This object can receive the label "bell," but not "car" or "airplane." It receives the label "bell" by virtue of the way the valid base functions. Mere labeling by mind is not enough—there has to be a valid base. In the case of a bell, the base has to have a certain shape and perform the function of ringing. This is what validates it.

Furthermore, the valid base that is merely labeled "bell" by the mind should not be harmed by another's valid mind. What's a valid mind? A mind that perceives things correctly, that is not under the influence of disease, drugs, mantras or hypnotic spells, which might cause it to see sense objects in an illusory way.

Next, the object we claim to exist should not be harmed by a fully enlightened being's mind. A buddha's mind is completely unmistaken, completely purified, free from hallucination. All existent phenomena are the object of the omniscient mind; it sees whatever exists. If the omniscient mind does not see the bell, the bell does not exist.

Finally, for the bell that is merely labeled by the mind to exist, it should not receive harm from the wisdom realizing emptiness, ultimate nature. If the bell, which is merely imputed by the mind, is harmed by the wisdom realizing emptiness, it does not exist. Thus, there are three kinds of mind that can harm, or invalidate, the existence of what appears to be, for example, a bell: another person's valid conventional mind; an omniscient mind; and the wisdom realizing emptiness.

Now, regarding this valid base, this phenomenon that has the function of ringing and possesses this particular shape, our mind creates the label, "bell." This, then, is the real bell, the bell that we use, the one that is merely imputed by our mind, the valid base that is labeled "bell" by our mind.

The worst ignorance

So what is the bell that does not exist? When your mind perceives the bell, it does not see a bell that is merely labeled by the mind. It sees something slightly beyond that, ever so slightly more than that. It sees something as existing from the side of the bell, something existing from its own side, from the side of the object. If you concentrate, if you analyze carefully how the bell exists, that it is merely labeled by the mind, you can see that there's nothing coming from the side of the bell. When you look deeply into the meaning of "merely labeled by the mind," you can see that nothing exists from the side of the object. When you concentrate on this, you can see how its existence comes only from your mind.

But the way the bell appears to us, the way we believe it exists, is slightly beyond its reality, slightly more than its actual mode of existence, which is being merely labeled by the mind. That's where the hallucination begins. Starting from there, the rest of the way it appears is a total hallucination. The way it appears, the way we believe it to exist—as something slightly beyond that which is merely labeled by the mind—is our biggest hallucination, the biggest suffering in the lives of us sentient beings. That's what keeps us continually circling in samsara, dying and being reborn, dying and being reborn, experiencing the same beginningless problems again and again.

There's no beginning to our experience of samsaric suffering and so far it has not ended. Why do we still suffer? Because we have not yet realized emptiness, the ultimate nature of phenomena—that things are empty, that things exist merely in name. We have not discovered reality; we have not discovered the wisdom that cuts the root of all delusion and karma, the true cause of suffering, the cause of samsara. We have not eradicated ignorance, the unknowing mind. We have continually been creating ignorance, the root of samsara. Instead of meditating on emptiness, practicing mindfulness, we have been making our mind more and more ignorant. That's why we continue to suffer.

So, what is this bell (or any other object you care to look at)? It is nothing other than that which is merely labeled by the mind. But our minds are so replete with negative imprints left by past ignorance, the simultaneously born concept of inherent existence, that even though things exist as merely labeled by the mind, we hold on to them as if they exist from their own side. We apprehend them as inherently existent, as not merely imputed by the mind.

Therefore, this bell is merely labeled by the mind. But because of

the negative imprints left on our mental continuum by past ignorance, the concept of inherent existence, the apprehension and belief
that phenomena exist from their own side, as soon as our mind creates the label "bell," as soon as it merely imputes "bell" on the base,
the negative imprints left on our mental continuum project the hallucination that it exists from its own side. It's like when you take a roll
of film to be developed—the images from the negative are projected
onto special paper, mixed with chemicals, and a picture appears to
make the photograph—or like putting a film into a projector and
beaming the images it contains onto a screen. Whatever the object—a
bell, your I—the moment it's labeled by the mind, the negative
imprints project upon it the adornment of inherent existence. The
thing is that we're unaware, or we forget, that what we're seeing is
merely imputed by our mind.

Basically, there are three things in the evolution of all this. First of
all, as a start, our mind merely labels the object. Second, the negative
imprints left by previous concepts of inherent existence project the
appearance of inherent existence that the object we're looking at now
exists from its own side, that there's a real bell there—not a bell from
our mind, but a bell from the side of the bell. This is a *totally, totally*
wrong idea—a complete hallucination projected onto the bell. Third,
we allow our mind to believe that this is one hundred percent true.
We allow our mind to hold on to this, to grasp this, as completely,
one hundred percent true—that there's a real bell over there, that
that's the reality.

This is ignorance. At that moment, we are making our mind ignorant, unknowing. We are making our mind ignorant as to the actual
nature of the bell, which in reality is totally empty from its own side.

What exists is merely labeled by the mind. The bell, which is totally empty from its own side, exists merely in name. Being unaware of this is an example of how we make our mind ignorant.

HALLUCINATION

Just as this applies to the example of the bell, so is it true for all other phenomena. Starting from our I, the way we see ourselves, everything we perceive is as hallucinated as our view of the bell. Our view is completely wrong and so too is the belief that we hold on to. Starting with the subject, I, whatever we perceive in the course of a twenty-four hour day does not exist the way in which we believe.

Think of everything we see during the course of one day; all the objects of form with which our eye sense comes into contact—shapes and colors, billions and billions of things wherever we look. No matter which of these billions of objects we observe, we see each one in just the same way as I described our view of the bell. Just as we don't see the bell as merely labeled by the mind, similarly, we don't see anything else we look at in its true nature, as merely labeled by the mind and totally empty from its own side. Even though, were we to analyze the bell's mode of existence logically, scientifically, we would understand the way in which it exists, that's not how we see it. The bell we see is something else altogether. In the same way, we misperceive every other object of form that appears to our eye consciousness. When we go into a supermarket or department store where even one section contains thousands of objects, we don't see even one of them in the way it exists. We're in a totally different world from the one that actually exists; our world is something else completely. What we see does not exist in the supermarket or the department store. In reality, what we see exists nowhere.

Everything we see is cloaked in hallucination. We go into a store and our mind labels things "this, this, this, this, this," but a layer of inherent existence completely covers all these objects merely labeled by mind. To us they appear as not merely labeled by mind, as existing from their own side—an appearance that is totally non-existent, a complete hallucination. This hallucination encases the entire world of form, a world that exists merely in name.

It's the same with sound. Before I was talking about forms, visual objects of the sense of eye. But we perceive much more than that. We have four other senses—hearing, smell, taste and touch. Thus, sounds also exist merely in name and not from their own side. But again, we hallucinate with every sound we hear, believing it to be inherently existent, when it's exactly the opposite. Every object of every sense exists merely in name, as a valid base merely labeled by the mind. But as long as we don't develop the wisdom realizing emptiness, we'll never see sense objects in their nature, the way they exist.

Instead, we cloak these merely labeled sense objects in the hallucination of existence from their own side and hang on to that as true, allow our mind to believe in our own hallucination that there really is something there. Because we do not practice mindfulness meditation on emptiness, or dependent arising—mindfulness on the hallucination that it is a hallucination—we constantly make our mind more and more ignorant.

For example, when we are dreaming, we can practice mindfulness that this is but a dream. Similarly, during the day, we can practice mindfulness that what we're seeing is but a hallucination. If we do

VIRTUE AND REALITY

this, we're not meditating that something that exists is a hallucination —we're meditating that a hallucination is a hallucination. As a result, what comes into our heart is an understanding of emptiness, the ultimate nature of the circle of three—I, action and object. By doing this, we stop making our mind increasingly ignorant. We stop constantly creating the basis for emotional thoughts, delusions, attachment—those unnecessary minds that bring no benefit, only harm, and motivate the karma that becomes the cause of samsara and all its realms of suffering.

WHAT IS THE MIND?

What's true for the physical senses, as above, is also true for the mind, the perceiver, itself. The mind is a phenomenon too. What is the mind? It is a phenomenon that is not body, not substantial, has no form, no shape, no color, but, like a mirror, can clearly reflect objects. Objects appear to the mind and the mind can perceive these objects. As long as a mirror is not dirty, it will reflect whatever object comes before it clearly. Similarly, since the mind is unobstructed by substance, form, objects can appear to it. The phenomenon that is mind perceives objects.

So, that is the base. In relation to that phenomenon, our thought creates, merely imputes, the label "mind," and that's how the mind exists. The mind also exists merely in name; what we call mind has been merely labeled by thought. It's like when a person is given a name. Mine is Zopa. Actually, it's Thubten Zopa, and it was given to me by my abbot. According to tradition, when an abbot ordains new monks, he gives them his first name. My abbot's first name was

Thubten, and then he added the Zopa. With his mind, he labeled me "Zopa." You received your name in a similar way. Whether you named yourself or it was given to you by your parents, your name is a mind-created label.

In the same way, then, what's called mind is also a name. We think there's a real mind—a real mind existing from there. That's how it appears to us and, without a shadow of doubt, we believe one hundred percent in this appearance. But if we analyze this phenomenon called mind, it's no different from the name given to you by your parents, which was created by their minds. What you call mind has been merely labeled by your thought in relation to its base, that formless phenomenon that has neither shape nor color, whose nature is clear and that has the ability to perceive objects. That is the base, and "mind" is the label. They're two distinct phenomena, not one. They're not separate, but they're different. That's what we have to realize—that these two phenomena are different. This is what we have to discover through meditation. By doing this we can begin to free ourselves from the hallucination that is the root of all suffering. This is how we start to liberate ourselves from samsara.

SCHOOLS OF BUDDHIST PHILOSOPHY AND THE OBJECT OF REFUTATION

I started this discussion by saying how everything exists as merely labeled by mind, and then went on to clarify that simply labeling things is not enough to bring them into existence, that just because something is merely labeled, does not mean it exists. Then I went on to mention the three things required for something to exist: a valid base, not receiving harm from another's valid mind, and not receiving harm from the wisdom realizing emptiness.

Now, going back to the bell. As I mentioned before, the way the bell appears to us and the way in which we believe it to exist are slightly beyond the way it actually exists, which is in mere name, as merely labeled by the mind. This difference is a very subtle hallucination that, in Buddhist philosophical teachings, is called the "object to be refuted," or the "object of refutation."

There are four schools of Buddhist philosophy—Vaibashika (*che-tra-mra-wa*), Sautrantika (*do-de-pa*), Cittamatra (*sem-tsam*) and Madhyamika (*u-ma-pa*). The fourth of these is the Middle Way school and is divided into two: Svatantrika (*rang-gyu-pa*) and Prasangika (*thal-gyur-wa*).

According to the Prasangika school, the object of refutation (or negation, *gag-cha*) is an extremely subtle object that is ever so slightly more than—a little over and above—what is merely labeled by the mind. The object of refutation is what appears to us; it is that in which we believe.

In order to attain liberation from the entire round of suffering and its cause, we need to cut its very root, the fundamental ignorance that keeps us in it. Of the many kinds of ignorance, which is the specific one that we have to eradicate? It is not the concept that believes the bell to exist the way it appears, which is what the texts usually describe as the root of samsara—except that in the case of the root of samsara, we should be talking about the I, not the bell that I've been using as an example here.

When the I appears to us, we believe that there is something slightly over and above what is merely labeled by the mind and that this is how the I exists. Then we believe that this is one hundred percent true and let our mind hold on to that. It is this specific, particular ignorance that is the root of all delusion, karma and suffering. This very one. It's not just any type of ignorance—it's this one.

As well as this kind of ignorance, there's the one described by the second Madhyamika school, the Svatantrika—the hallucination on the I, the object to be refuted according to their view. I'm just mentioning this so that you'll have an idea of how trapped our minds are, how many different levels of ignorance we experience, how many kinds of hallucination there are. The hallucination on the I that the Svatantrikas describe is grosser than the one the Prasangikas explain. Then there's the Cittamatrins' version, where they say that the I exists from its own side without depending on mental imprints, without the mind as creator. They describe a seventh level of consciousness— normally we talk about just six—that is called the basis of samsara and nirvana. So they say that the I exists totally from its own side without depending on imprints left on this seventh level of consciousness and describe it as a self-entity.

According to Hindu philosophy, the I, which they call *atman,* is permanent. While the self is actually impermanent, they believe it to be permanent. Therefore, there's a lot of discussion in Buddhist texts refuting this view, explaining that while the self may appear to us to be permanent, in fact it changes moment by moment due to causes and conditions and is therefore impermanent. If you look at your I right now, you'll see that it appears to be permanent, whereas you know that in reality it is impermanent in nature.

Other views hold, for example, that while the I is dependent upon parts, there is the appearance and the belief that it exists alone, not dependent upon parts, or that while the I is dependent upon causes and conditions, there is the appearance and the belief that it exists with its own freedom, without depending on causes and conditions. These gross hallucinations are described and posited as the object of refutation by the first Buddhist school, the Vaibashika. This school has eighteen divisions, each with its own variant view. Then there's the hallucination that even though the I exists dependent upon the group and continuity of the aggregates, it appears to us as a self-entity existing without depending on the group and continuity of the aggregates. So these are some of the positions held by the Vaibashika and the Sautrantika, the lower Buddhist schools.

How has it come about that there are these four schools of Buddhist philosophy? It's due to the different ways of explaining what the I is. In reality, emptiness is just one, not many. There is only one emptiness that directly cuts the root of samsara. This is the emptiness taught by the Prasangika-Madhyamika school, whose view of emptiness is the unmistaken, pure one and the only one that can cut the specific ignorance that I mentioned before.

However, not everybody has the karma to accept this, to understand this, to realize this. Sentient beings have different levels of mind. Therefore, the all-knowing, kind, compassionate Buddha taught varying levels of philosophy to guide sentient beings' minds gradually up to the level where they could realize the Prasangika view of emptiness. One could start with the gross explanations of emptiness taught by the lower schools and gradually progress up to the most subtle, the Prasangika. That's how the four schools came into being. The lower schools were steps to the higher ones, leading ultimately to the Prasangika. So even though the views of these various schools seem to contradict each other, actually they're a method for gradually developing through study and meditation the Prasangika view.

HOW TO MEDITATE ON EMPTINESS

In case you are interested in practicing meditation on emptiness, I'm going to explain a couple of simple but quite helpful techniques for doing so.

The first technique is one that I often mention during meditation courses—walking meditation on emptiness. This is a kind of mindfulness meditation but it's much more profound than the usual mindfulness of walking where you simply maintain awareness of "I'm walking" and so forth. If you can practice that kind of mindfulness of walking—"I'm walking"—you can also practice mindfulness of stealing while robbing a bank or picking somebody's pocket—"I'm stealing." Actually, if you are stealing, it's probably not such a bad idea to be mindful—otherwise you might get caught!

Mindfulness meditation should be more than just watching what you are doing. What you really need to watch is your motivation. If you don't watch your mind, you don't know what's motivating your actions. What you should be doing is detecting negative motivation, the cause of suffering, and changing it into positive. You should be applying your meditation like a medicine to the eradication of harmful thoughts, the delusions—the disturbing emotions that harm yourself and others. You need to eradicate these and make your mind healthy and your attitude beneficial, just as the Buddha explained in the verse I quoted before:

Do not engage in any harmful actions;

Perform only those that are good....

Abandon non-virtue, the cause of suffering, and practice virtue, the cause of happiness. Transform negative motivation into positive so that your actions will become virtuous. In this way you will not waste your life but make it meaningful. At least you won't be harming yourself or others.

The way to practice more meaningful mindfulness is this. For example, when you're sitting or when you're walking, ask yourself the question, "What am I doing?" Then your mind will answer, "I'm sitting," "I'm walking," "I'm eating," depending on what it is that you're doing. "I'm cooking," "I'm talking." Whatever you are doing, you can meditate on emptiness.

One way in which you can do this is to reply to the answer "I'm walking" with another question: "Why do I say 'I'm walking'?" Then you analyze; you look for the reason. What you find is, "The only reason I say this is that my aggregate of body, the base I label "I," is walking." Your body is walking—just because of that, your mind labels and believes "I'm walking."

After you've done that, check how your I appears to you at that moment. Is it the same as before or has there been a change? Usually you'll find that it's not the same, that there's been a definite change. Suddenly, the old view of a real I in your body, appearing from that side, the I you have always believed to be there in your body, has vanished, become non-existent. And that's the truth. It's not a false view. The old I was the false one. When you do not meditate, do not analyze, the I that appears to you and in which you believe—the I that seems to be on these aggregates, in this body—is the false one. In philosophical texts, we refer to that I as inherently existent or existing by nature. In Western psychological terms, we call it the "emotional I." The emotional I—the one that you believe is in your body or on your aggregates—is totally non-existent. That is what you have to discover— that it's empty. You have to discover that it is totally non-existent, totally empty.

If you can realize that—that there's not even the slightest atom of an I there—and feel as if you yourself have become totally non-existent, you have entered the Middle Way. At that time, when you realize emptiness, you gain full conviction, or definite understanding, that you can attain liberation, you can cease all suffering and its cause.

Remain in the state of your discovery of the absence of the emotional I. Keep your mind in the emptiness of that. When your mind gets distracted, again ask yourself the question, "What am I doing?" Then, when your mind replies, ask again, "Why do I say 'I'm doing...'? There's no reason other than...," whatever it is. If the answer is, "I'm meditating," ask yourself, "Why do I say 'I'm meditating'?" There's no reason other than the fact that the base, the aggregates of mind, are transforming into virtue (which is what meditation really means). Then check again to see what effect this has had on your I. Has there been a change or not?

Doing this meditation again and again helps you see the false I more and more clearly. The more clearly you see the false I, the emotional I, the I that doesn't exist, the more clearly you see, the better you recognize, emptiness—the better idea of emptiness you get.

The second technique for meditating on emptiness is one that takes you back to your childhood, to the time before you had learned the alphabet. Imagine yourself before you knew your ABCs. You're sitting in the classroom and your teacher draws a letter on the blackboard for the first time. You, the child, have no idea what it is, what those lines represent. Although the teacher draws an A, you have no appearance of A. Even though you see the lines on the blackboard, A does not appear to you. You see the lines but you don't see them as A. That's because your mind hasn't labeled those lines as A and believed in that. Remember, labeling is not enough—in order for there to be appearance, you have to believe in it as well. At this point in your life, your mind has not yet labeled that configuration and believed, "This is an A."

Then your teacher tells you, "This is an A," and your mind—believing what your teacher has said, in relation to that base, those lines on the blackboard—creates the label A, merely imputes it on the base, and believes in it. Only then do you have the appearance of the letter A. After that, then you see that this is an A.

The point to understand here is that first there's that arrangement of lines, which is the base. What is it that makes your mind decide upon the particular label A? You don't label any old configuration A—it has to be this particular pattern. That's why your mind chooses to label it A—it sees the appropriate pattern. That is the base; the base to be labeled A.

So you can see that the base, that particular pattern, and the label are different. This is the point I'm trying to make. The pattern is the base and the A is the label. These are two different phenomena, not one. They appear as one—without analysis, to your mind they appear as one. It looks as if the A is on top of the base, that pattern. It looks like that. If you do not analyze, it appears as if the A were right there, on that pattern, as if the A were there on that base.

So, the pattern is the base and the A is the label. Now you need to concentrate on the conclusion. Before your mind creates the label A, you see the base, that particular pattern, first. That's what causes you to apply the label A. From this it's clear that the base is not the A. If it were, you should see the A at the very first moment you saw the base, but that isn't what happens. It doesn't happen no matter what phenomenon you see. First you see the base; then you apply the label. Your mind creates the label after seeing the base.

Taking a pillar, for example—the specific base that holds things up, that performs that particular function—seeing that base first causes your mind to choose the label "pillar." Then you see the pillar. You don't see it from the very beginning. If you saw the base but your mind didn't label it, you wouldn't see the pillar.

Similarly, you see the A later. That means that the pattern and the A are not one. The pattern is not A—it is the base to be labeled A. This is the point to understand. The difference between the two. This is one line of reasoning.

A second line of reasoning goes as follows. Look for the A. On that pattern, where is the A? Look at the upstroke (/). You don't find the A there. Look at the downstroke (\). It's not there either. Nor is the A on the crossbar (-). Even when the three lines are assembled into the configuration A, that's not the A because that's the base to be labeled. Only after seeing it do you label it A. So the three lines together are not the A either.

So when you see that three-line pattern on a blackboard, there's no A on the pattern, but there's an A on the blackboard, and the only reason you can say that, is that the pattern is on the blackboard.

Similarly, when you look out of your window and see a car go by, analyze what happens. First of all, before anything appears, you don't label "car" because you haven't seen anything. There's no reason for you to label, "There goes a car." When a car does go by, you don't label it "car" the very moment you see it because for your mind to choose that particular label, "car," you have to see something first, as we've been saying. What causes your mind to create the label? There has to be a prior reason. You have to see something *before* you create the label. What you see is the base—the phenomenon that has the appropriate shape and performs the function of going here and there, transporting people and so forth—you have to see that first. The label "car" comes after that. First you see the base; then you see the car. You see the car after you have applied the label. Therefore, it is a hallucination. Whatever you see go by—a person, a cat, a dog, a motorcycle—it works the same way.

Under normal circumstances, when we do not analyze what we see, when a car goes by it looks as if either the base itself is the car or there's a car on that base, and we think that is what's going by. This is a complete hallucination. There's no car there, just as there's no A on that configuration of three lines. The car exists but it's not there.

It's the same thing with the A. When we look at the A and do not analyze, do not meditate, it looks as if the A is *there,* on that pattern. That too is a complete hallucination. That is the object to be refuted— the A that is there not merely imputed by the mind. An A that if you look for it can not be found. That's the object of refutation; that's what we have to realize is empty. And that emptiness is the ultimate nature of the A.

The reason that seeing an A on the base is a false view is that if you try to find precisely where on each of the three lines it is (/\-), you can't find it. And when you look for it on the three lines assembled (A), you can't find it there either. Each piece is not A; and neither is the assembled pattern, because that is the base to be labeled A.

By analyzing in this way, you can recognize your everyday hallucinations, your false view, and understand what you have to realize as empty. What emptiness means. Analysis makes it clear. Practicing mindfulness of this, meditating on this, helps you to control your emotional mind. It becomes almost impossible for emotional thoughts, such as attachment and anger, to arise. That means you stop motivating karma, the cause of samsara, the cause of the lower realms. Thus it becomes incredible protection, a great source of happiness and peace, and the cause of liberation and enlightenment for yourself and all other sentient beings. By developing this wisdom and practicing bodhicitta, you yourself can attain enlightenment and lead all other sentient beings to enlightenment as well.

Therefore, if you really want to practice Dharma, meditate, and see some development in your life, if you want to clarify and deepen your understanding of emptiness and bring yourself closer to realizing it, these techniques might help, even though they don't utilize philosophical concepts, the four-point analysis and so forth. By practicing these techniques, you can see more clearly how the mind is not I, which is what many people think. Many things become clear.

Practicing the Good Heart

The practice of compassion, the good heart, is incredibly important. We really need compassion. Compassion is the source of all our happiness.

Every single happiness that you experience in your life, every single comfort and enjoyment of your daily life, as well as the everlasting happiness of liberation and the bliss of highest enlightenment, comes from bodhicitta. The root of bodhicitta is great compassion. Thus, whatever happiness you experience derives from great compassion. Then, your bringing happiness to all sentient beings—the happiness of this life, the happiness of future lives, the everlasting happiness of liberation and enlightenment—depends upon your having compassion for yourself. It all has to come from your own compassion. Therefore, compassion is the most important human quality in which you can educate your mind.

When do we need compassion?

In every life situation, you need compassion. When you live with your family, you need compassion. Without compassion, your family life is full of problems and suffering. When you do business, you need compassion. Otherwise you experience so much frustration, unhappiness and dissatisfaction. If you're a doctor or a nurse working in a hospital you need compassion. If you don't have compassion, your job becomes boring, tiring, exhausting and uninteresting—because you are motivated by only the wish for your own happiness. You're trying to do something for others but it becomes just a job.

When teaching in school, you need compassion. When studying, the best way to learn is with compassion. In that way, your study becomes meaningful; beneficial for other sentient beings. Your life becomes beneficial for others; your study becomes service for other sentient beings. Whatever your lifestyle—singing, dancing, acting, theater—what makes it meaningful is having compassion for others. That transforms it into service for others. Even in the army you need compassion. In that way you can make your actions transcendent, special, out of the ordinary. With compassion for others, instead of being negative, your actions can become virtuous, the cause of enlightenment, a means of purifying negative karma and gathering merit. Even an action such as killing, if done with very strong compassion, strong bodhicitta, can become a cause for enlightenment; not just a cause for enlightenment but a powerful, rapid cause for enlightenment—if done with strong bodhicitta, totally renouncing yourself to suffer for the sake of others.

Even if you're a prostitute, if you are motivated by compassion, by bodhicitta, your life is not ordinary. Your life becomes transcendent; your deeds those of a bodhisattva. No matter what you do, if your motivation is out of the ordinary, great compassion, bodhicitta, your life becomes meaningful, beneficial for others. There's no risk, no danger.

Similarly, if you are in retreat, what makes your retreat most beneficial, extremely effective and highly meaningful is if you do it with compassion for others, and the stronger your compassion, the more powerful a purification it becomes.

And not only in retreat. Even if in your everyday life you do your prayers and sadhanas—even a rosary of mantras—with compassion for others, each mantra you recite becomes highly meaningful, beneficial for all beings. The stronger your compassion, the more powerful each mantra. Each little mantra can have the power of an atomic bomb. Nuclear weapons are so small but they can destroy so much. Like that, even short mantras, when done with strong compassion, can purify the karma of having killed human beings. One repetition of the mantra OM MANI PADME HUNG motivated by strong compassion can purify the negative karma of the ten non-virtuous actions. One repetition of this mantra can purify a fully ordained monk's having committed all four defeats, the violation of his four root vows—killing a human being, lying about realizations he doesn't have, engaging in sexual intercourse and stealing something that was not given—even one of which is extremely heavy.

Even if you are trying to work for others by doing social service, if you have no compassion many problems can arise, such as personality clashes with your colleagues because of strong egos, anger and so forth. Even offering service to others can cause problems if you don't have a good heart, compassion. That's because you are motivated by ego, the self-centered mind. This inevitably causes problems to arise, creates obstacles to the work going smoothly and prevents you from enjoying your work or your colleagues. Eventually you have to leave because you can't stand it any longer.

Far beyond our level, similar principles apply. Maitreya Buddha generated bodhicitta, became a bodhisattva, much earlier than Guru Shakyamuni Buddha did, yet Guru Shakyamuni Buddha became enlightened before Maitreya. Before becoming a buddha, you have to become a bodhisattva. First you have to realize renunciation of samsara, your own samsara. Then you generate compassion for the samsaric suffering of others using your own suffering as an example. Your compassion for other sentient beings—wishing them to be free of all suffering and to have all happiness, including that of enlightenment—leads you to the decision to bring about all sentient beings' enlightenment by yourself.

HOW TO ENLIGHTEN ALL SENTIENT BEINGS

At the moment, you can't guide even one sentient being to enlightenment. In order to be able to work perfectly on behalf of them all—to free them from all suffering and bring them to full enlightenment—you have to complete your own mind training in compassion. You also have to develop perfect power, so that you can reveal to all sentient beings the appropriate methods according to their level of mind. Finally, you must become omniscient, having the ability to read every single thought of the numberless sentient beings and know all their characteristics, such as their level of intelligence and the details of their karma, and what methods suit each one at any given time. You have to know all these things directly. In other words, without first attaining enlightenment yourself, without becoming a buddha yourself, you cannot do perfect, unmistaken work for sentient beings.

Even arhants, who have completed the five paths, cannot work perfectly for sentient beings because they lack omniscient mind. They can still make mistakes when guiding others. To attain enlightenment according to sutra, you pass through five paths and ten bhumis. Even a tenth level bodhisattva, someone on the brink of enlightenment, can make a mistake when it comes to helping others, because his or her mind is not omniscient. Therefore, to best help others, you must first become omniscient; you *must* first become a buddha.

The root of enlightenment, omniscience, and all the realizations of the Mahayana path is bodhicitta. Bodhicitta is the gateway to the Mahayana path to enlightenment. In order to realize bodhicitta, you need its root, great compassion. Therefore, it is essential that you achieve this realization, and to do so, you must live your life with compassion.

Now, as I said before, Maitreya Buddha generated bodhicitta long before Guru Shakyamuni Buddha did, but Guru Shakyamuni Buddha got enlightened first. How did this happen? Because Guru Shakyamuni Buddha's bodhicitta, his great compassion, was much stronger than Maitreya Buddha's. The story of this goes back many, many lifetimes, when in a previous life they were brothers living in Nepal. One day, the two brothers came across a family of five tigers who were dying of starvation. They both felt compassion, of course, but Guru Shakyamuni Buddha's must have been much stronger, because later he came back to the tigers alone and offered them his body, sacrificing his life in order to save theirs. Later, after Guru Shakyamuni Buddha had attained enlightenment, because of the karmic connection made with the tigers when he was a bodhisattva, they were reborn human and became his first disciples. He taught them Dharma and they achieved realizations of the path.

While Maitreya Buddha and Guru Shakyamuni Buddha both saw

the tigers and felt compassion, Maitreya Buddha did not make charity of his body as did Guru Shakyamuni Buddha. This shows that Shakyamuni's bodhicitta was much stronger. Thus, he was able to sacrifice himself for others that much more, and as a result, attained enlightenment first.

We should be guided by Guru Shakyamuni Buddha's example in our daily lives and understand that the stronger our compassion, the more we can sacrifice our lives for others, the greater the amount of negative karma we can purify and the more merit we can accumulate. With strong compassion, we can purify unbelievably vast amounts of negative karma and generate merit as vast as space itself. Like Guru Shakyamuni Buddha, the more we can dedicate our daily lives to others with compassion, the sooner we will attain enlightenment. This is the way to benefit from the life histories of the great bodhisattvas and yogis. We should learn from and follow their example. In that way we'll become enlightened sooner and be able to enlighten all sentient beings more quickly. Thus, those who need our help, those who are depending on us to alleviate their suffering, won't have to wait so long, won't have to suffer so much. The sooner, the more strongly, we can develop compassion and bodhicitta, the sooner we'll achieve the other realizations of the path and the sooner we'll reach enlightenment. Thus, we'll be able to reach our actual goal—the liberation from suffering and the enlightenment of all sentient beings—more quickly, thus realizing the real meaning of our lives and fulfilling our actual purpose.

However, generating compassion in your daily life has more immediate benefits as well. If you have compassion, you have fewer problems. With compassion, the problems you do experience are experienced for the sake of others, and thus become the path to enlightenment. Experiencing problems becomes a means for happiness for both yourself and others. In this way, with compassion, you transform problems into happiness.

Compassion also helps you prepare for death. The best way to die is with bodhicitta, feeling great compassion for other sentient beings. That's a high quality death—dying with compassion for others. By dying with compassion, you have no fear or worry. You're experiencing death for others. It becomes simply a change of body, like trading old clothes for new. When you die with compassion you're simply trading your old body for a new one.

Thus, living with compassion completely changes your life. It transforms an ordinary life into a transcendent one. It elevates everything you do. Your entire life becomes totally different; highly meaningful; your heart is full. Your heart is not empty and neither is your life.

Therefore, you must think, "Compassion is the source of not only all my happiness but that of all sentient beings as well. It is the source of all happiness, including that of enlightenment. In order to offer all this happiness to others, I need to generate compassion myself."

DEVELOPING COMPASSION

However, merely saying, "I need compassion" is not enough. You have to understand the teachings on how to develop compassion. That means that first you have to study, and then practice, meditate. In that way you can achieve realizations. Thus, you need to listen to teachings.

In order to develop compassion, to realize compassion for other sentient beings, so that you can realize bodhicitta, the gateway to the Mahayana path to enlightenment, you need the preliminary realization of renunciation. Renunciation is the determination to be free from your own samsara, which you must realize to be totally in the nature of suffering. You must feel your own samsara to be a blazing fire, with yourself in the middle of it, such that you can't bear to remain in it for a moment longer. You need to generate such strong aversion to samsara that the wish to be rid of it arises spontaneously, day and night, just as a prisoner wishes constantly, day and night, to be released from jail. As a prisoner finds not even a second's attraction to prison, that's how you should feel about your own samsara. You should feel it to be as desirable as a pit of rattlesnakes—a place that you have not the slightest wish to be in, even for a second, and if you are in it, not the slightest wish to remain for a moment longer. This is how you must feel about your own samsara. This is renunciation.

In order to renounce your own samsara, first you have to feel detached from this life. Only with detachment from this life can you practice Dharma purely. Renunciation of this life is the preliminary understanding you need before you can develop renunciation from the whole of your samsara. In order to develop great compassion for all sentient beings, you need these preliminary realizations. Compassion doesn't just drop into your brain from the sky or appear in your mind the moment you read about it. Compassion and bodhicitta have to be developed in a step-by-step manner by gradually developing the preliminary realizations in their logical order.

THE IMPORTANCE OF THE MEDITATION CENTER

So now you can see the necessity of the meditation center, a place where people can study teachings on how to develop compassion; an organization established for the purpose of offering instructions in the development of the good heart. Compassion, the good heart, is extremely important, but you have to learn how to acquire it. You have to study the whole path. Therefore, it is essential that there be places that give people the opportunity to study all of the Buddha's teachings—not just the part about compassion but the entire path to enlightenment; every aspect of method and wisdom.

The essence of Buddhism is compassion for all without discrimination, and on that basis, not giving harm. Not harming others, and as well as that, benefiting all. Compassion for not only your friends but your enemies too. Compassion for all without exception: friends, enemies and strangers. This is what Buddhism is all about.

Therefore, every person who comes to a Dharma center to study the teachings of the Buddha and to learn to meditate will be taught how to develop compassion for others. That means each of these people will stop harming sentient beings, stop giving harm to the world. In other words, numberless other sentient beings, people in the world, people in each country, will not be harmed by each person who comes to the center to study the Dharma and practice compassion. Thus, numberless other sentient beings receive much peace and happiness from each of these people.

By hearing the teachings of the Buddha, especially the lamrim—teachings on subduing the mind, taking care of the mind, protecting your mind and the minds of others—the steps of the path to enlightenment, whether it's a one-week course, a weekend course, a one-day teaching or even a single lecture, the emphasis is usually on karma or compassion. The essence of the subject is usually not to harm others and on that basis, to benefit them as much as possible. So usually people will come away from even a few hours of teaching with the understanding that they should at least not harm others.

Therefore, even though such people may not be able to do all those traditional practices—many sadhanas, mantra recitation, preliminary practices, lam-rim meditation—at least when they see ants or other insects on the floor they won't step on them. Even if they don't do any of those other practices, at least they'll have the thought in their minds not to kill insects, worms and so forth. At least that one minimum practice will be there. That itself is a great benefit. Even if they can't do anything else, at least they're thinking, "It is really wrong to kill, to harm another's life."

In this way, there's much peace for many animals and insects and for that person as well. The person creates less negative karma and therefore does not have to experience the suffering results that would otherwise have ripened in life after life. So, the absence of that is peace. That numberless other sentient beings—animals, insects, other humans—don't receive harm from each of these people who stop killing after they have come to the center, is just one of the extensive benefits that the center offers. On top of that, of course, are all the teachings and meditation on the lam-rim, emptiness, bodhicitta, the preliminary practices and so forth. But just stopping killing itself is highly beneficial; it brings much happiness to many others.

Before the Kalachakra initiation by His Holiness the Dalai Lama in Australia in 1996, I spent a month in retreat at a student's house near the ocean. Every day I went to the beach to do a practice where you make charity of water to the pretas. You recite a special mantra, which blesses the water, and then offer them the water, which the pretas receive as nectar. The entire expanse of water appears to them as nectar, which purifies their minds and they get liberated from the lower realms and receive a good rebirth. When I was there I would see many people fishing. It wasn't that they were hungry; they did it out of enjoyment. They would either go out in boats or stand at the water's edge with their lines in the water for hours at a time. So many fish would lose their lives. However, if one person who likes to fish comes to a teaching at the center and as a result of hearing about karma and compassion stops killing, the lives of so many fish are saved, not to mention those of all the other animals and insects that the person refrains from harming.

If a person does not change his mind, change his actions, so many sentient beings will have to suffer during the course of his life, as will he, in many future lives, from the horrible karma he creates. But if this person comes to the center and stops killing, for as many more months and years as he continues to live, others receive that much more peace and happiness. From the opposite point of view, the person who dies not having had the opportunity to hear the Buddha-dharma or to change his mind, the longer he lives, the more harm he gives to others and himself.

In order to develop compassion, bodhicitta, meditation is not enough. You need to receive the blessing of the special deity of compassion, Chenrezig (Avalokiteshvara). Then your meditation on the path will be more effective in bringing you to the realization of compassion. In Tibet and other Himalayan countries, many people recite

OM MANI PADME HUNG, the mantra of Chenrezig. Many of them are simple people who have very limited intellectual understanding of the teachings or can't even read, but wherever they go—while working, traveling, at home—they constantly recite this mantra. Just because of this and their devotion and prayers to the Compassionate Buddha, Chenrezig, they tend to be naturally very compassionate, very warm-hearted, always more concerned for others than themselves, wanting to help others and give them things.

For example, a few years ago my mother passed away, aged 84. She reincarnated as a boy in Nepal, near where she had lived, with a very clear memory of people and things from his previous life. One reason she was able to reincarnate as a human being with a clear mind and the ability to remember so much was because she used to recite 50,000 OM MANI PADME HUNG mantras every day, almost up until the time she died. She was also a nun for the last seventeen years of her life, living in the pure morality of her ordination. Because of all this, she was able to reincarnate as a human being with the opportunity to practice Dharma once again.

Dharma centers are of utmost importance in the world today. They give people the opportunity to learn about karma and compassion. World peace depends upon people having loving kindness and compassion. If people don't have compassion, life becomes very dangerous. Therefore, we need places where the methods for developing compassion are taught. This is where you learn; this is where you give others the chance to learn as well. Peace through weapons is extremely unreliable, but peace without force, through people changing their minds by generating compassion, by choice, with freedom, is of benefit to the country, to the world, to all sentient beings. Therefore, even for peace in the country itself, meditation centers, where the essential practice is that of compassion and people are taught how to bring peace, are indispensable.

Therefore, members of Dharma organizations ought to know all these benefits that I have just explained, from the minimum—people stop killing—all the way up to enlightenment. Everybody who contributes to the center in any way is giving enlightenment to others, helping them find liberation from suffering and giving them good rebirths by helping them understand karma. In short, offering peace and happiness to many. However many members a center has, that many people are making this incredible contribution to the world. All these benefits come from every person who helps the center exist, develop and do its work. So it's good to be aware of and remember this and to enjoy the benefits. Therefore, I would like to request everyone to continue with their own practice and to continue helping their center for the sake of other sentient beings.

DEDICATION

The reason that we dedicate the merit generated by any virtuous activity is in order to protect it from destruction by negative forces, such as anger or wrong views, and to direct it toward the goal that we always specify in our motivation—the enlightenment of all sentient beings. You can use the elaborate dedication given below whenever you have created merit of any kind. Just pause for a moment after each paragraph and meditate on its meaning.

Please dedicate the merit of having read and practiced the teachings in this book as follows:

"Due to the past, present and future merit accumulated by myself and all buddhas, bodhisattvas and other sentient beings, may bodhicitta arise in my mind and in the minds of all members of my family and all other sentient beings, and may the bodhicitta that has already arisen in our minds only increase more and more.

"Due to the merits of the past, present and future, may His Holiness the Dalai Lama's life be stable and may his holy wishes succeed immediately. May all our gurus' lives be stable and may all their holy wishes succeed immediately. May Lama Ösel Rinpoche's life be stable and may he be able to offer benefit as vast as space itself to all sentient beings and to the teachings of the Buddha, just as Lama Tsong Khapa was able to do.

"Due to the past, present and future merit accumulated by myself and all buddhas, bodhisattvas and other sentient beings, may I and all the other students of the FPMT (or whatever Dharma organization you belong to), all the benefactors, all the members of (insert the name of your Dharma center), everybody else who comes here to study, and all the rest of the sentient beings, in this and all future lifetimes, be able to meet only perfectly qualified Mahayana gurus, see them only as enlightened beings, act in ways that only please the holy minds of our virtuous friends, and be able to fulfill their holy wishes.

"Due to the past, present and future merit accumulated by myself and all buddhas, bodhisattvas and other sentient beings, may I be able to offer benefit as vast as space itself to all sentient beings and to the teachings of the Buddha, just as Lama Tsong Khapa was able to do, by developing all his holy qualities within myself in this and all future lifetimes.

"Due to the past, present and future merit accumulated by myself and all buddhas, bodhisattvas and other sentient beings, all of which are empty from their own side, may the I, which is also empty from its own side, achieve Guru Shakyamuni Buddha's enlightenment, which is also empty from its own side, and lead all sentient beings, who are empty from their own side, to that enlightenment, which is empty from its own side, by myself alone, which is also empty from its own side.

"Due to the past, present and future merit accumulated by myself and all buddhas, bodhisattvas and other sentient beings, may my Dharma center (mention its name) be able to fulfill all sentient beings' wishes, immediately pacify the sufferings of their body and mind, spread the complete teachings of Lama Tsong Khapa throughout the minds of all sentient beings, and receive all conditions necessary to do so. May all who come to the center, even animals, insects and spirits, by just entering the place, never again be reborn in the lower realms, immediately purify all their obscurations and negative karma, be free of all sickness and harm from malevolent spirits, immediately actualize bodhicitta, and attain enlightenment as quickly as possible. May this come to pass at all other FPMT centers as well.

"May all members of this center and all benefactors, students and other people connected with the FPMT, particularly those who sacrifice their lives in service of others and the teaching of the Buddha, have long and healthy lives, have all their Dharma wishes come true, and, especially, actualize the entire path to enlightenment in this very life.

"May Lama Tsong Khapa's teachings exist and flourish in all directions until samsara ends. May all projects of the FPMT, especially the 500 foot Maitreya statue at Bodhgaya, receive all necessary conditions, actualize immediately, and, most importantly, be of greatest benefit to all sentient beings, causing them to actualize loving kindness, compassion and bodhicitta. Through this, may all war, famine, disease, earthquakes and all other natural disasters and undesired experiences never occur, and, like the rising sun, may all beings enjoy the happiness of Dharma and spend their entire lives only helping, never harming, each other. May we all attain enlightenment as quickly as possible."

THE LAMA YESHE WISDOM ARCHIVE

The LAMA YESHE WISDOM ARCHIVE (LYWA) is the collected works of Lama Thubten Yeshe and Lama Thubten Zopa Rinpoche. The ARCHIVE was founded in 1996 by Lama Zopa Rinpoche, its spiritual director, to make available in various ways the teachings it contains. Distribution of free booklets of edited teachings is one of the ways.

Lama Yeshe and Lama Zopa Rinpoche began teaching at Kopan Monastery, Nepal, in 1970. Since then, their teachings have been recorded and transcribed. At present the LYWA contains about 6,000 cassette tapes and approximately 40,000 pages of transcribed teachings on computer disk. Many tapes by Lama Zopa Rinpoche remain to be transcribed. As Rinpoche continues to teach, the number of tapes in the ARCHIVE increases accordingly. Most of the transcripts have been neither checked nor edited.

Here at the LYWA we are making every effort to organize the transcription of that which has not yet been transcribed, to edit that which has not yet been edited, and generally to do the many other tasks detailed below. In all this, we need your help. Please contact us for more information.

THE LAMA YESHE WISDOM ARCHIVE
PO Box 356
Weston, MA 02493, USA
Telephone (781) 899-9587
email nribush@cs.com
www.LamaYeshe.com

THE ARCHIVE TRUST

The work of the LAMA YESHE WISDOM ARCHIVE falls into two categories: archiving and dissemination.

ARCHIVING requires managing the audiotapes of teachings by Lama Yeshe and Lama Zopa Rinpoche that have already been collected, collecting tapes of teachings given but not yet sent to the ARCHIVE, and collecting tapes of Lama Zopa's on-going teachings, talks, advice and so forth as he travels the world for the benefit of all. Tapes are then catalogued and stored safely while being kept accessible for further work.

We organize the transcription of tapes, add the transcripts to the already existent database of teachings, manage this database, have transcripts checked, and make transcripts available to editors or others doing research on or practicing these teachings.

Other archiving activities include working with videotapes and photographs of the Lamas and investigating the latest means of preserving ARCHIVE materials.

DISSEMINATION involves making the Lamas' teachings available directly or indirectly through various avenues such as booklets for free distribution, regular books for the trade, lightly edited transcripts, floppy disks, audio- and videotapes, and articles in *Mandala* and other magazines, and on the LYWA Web site, www.LamaYeshe.com. Irrespective of the method we choose, the teachings require a significant amount of work to prepare them for distribution.

This is just a summary of what we do. The ARCHIVE was established with virtually no seed funding and has developed solely through the kindness of many people, some of whom we have mentioned at the front of this booklet.

Our further development similarly depends upon the generosity of those who see the benefit and necessity of this work, and we would be extremely grateful for your help.

THE ARCHIVE TRUST has been established to fund the above activities and we hereby appeal to you for your kind support. If you would like to make a contribution to help us with any of the above tasks or to sponsor booklets for free distribution, please contact us at the address above.

The LAMA YESHE WISDOM ARCHIVE is a 501(c)(3) tax-deductible, non-profit corporation (ID number 04-3374479) dedicated to the welfare of all sentient beings and totally dependent upon your donations for its continued existence.

Thank you so much for your support. You may contribute by mailing us a check, bank draft or money order to our Weston address, by mailing us or phoning in your credit card number, or by transferring funds directly to our bank—details below. Thank you so much.

Bank information

Name of bank: Fleet
ABA routing number 011000390
Account: LYWA 546-81495
SWIFT address: FNBB US 33

THE FOUNDATION FOR THE PRESERVATION OF THE MAHAYANA TRADITION

The Foundation for the Preservation of the Mahayana Tradition (FPMT) is an international organization of Buddhist meditation, study and retreat centers, both urban and rural, monasteries, publishing houses, healing centers and other related activities founded in 1975 by Lama Thubten Yeshe and Lama Thubten Zopa Rinpoche. At present, there are more than 120 FPMT activities in twenty-five countries worldwide.

The FPMT has been established to facilitate the study and practice of Mahayana Buddhism in general, and the Tibetan Gelug tradition, founded in the fifteenth century by the great scholar, yogi and saint, Lama Je Tsong Khapa, in particular, for the benefit of all sentient beings.

Every two months, the Foundation publishes a magazine, *Mandala*, from its international office in the United States of America. For a sample issue of the magazine or for more information about the organization, please contact:

FPMT
PO Box 800
Soquel, CA 95073, USA
Telephone (831) 476-8435; fax (831) 476-4823
email fpmt@compuserve.com
or check out our Web site at www.fpmt.org

Our Web site also offers teachings by His Holiness the Dalai Lama, Lama Yeshe, Lama Zopa Rinpoche and many other highly respected teachers in the tradition; details of the FPMT's educational programs; a complete listing of FPMT centers all over the world and in your area; back issues of *Mandala*; and links to FPMT centers on the web, where you will find details of their programs, and to other interesting Buddhist and Tibetan home pages.

Lama Zopa Rinpoche
Teachings from the Vajrasattva Retreat
Edited by Ailsa Cameron and Nicholas Ribush

This book is an edited transcript of Rinpoche's teachings during the Vajrasattva retreat at Land of Medicine Buddha, California, February through April, 1999. It contains explanations of the various practices done during the retreat, such as Vajrasattva purification, prostrations to the Thirty-five Buddhas, Lama Chöpa, making light offerings, liberating animals and much, much more. There are also many weekend public lectures covering general topics such as compassion and emptiness. The appendices detail several of the practices taught, for example, the short Vajrasattva sadhana, light offerings, liberating animals and making charity of water to Dzambhala and the pretas.

It is essential reading for all Lama Zopa Rinpoche's students, especially retreat leaders and FPMT center spiritual program coordinators, and serious Dharma students everywhere.

704 pp., detailed table of contents, 7 appendices
6" x 9" paperback
ISBN 1-891868-04-7
US$20 & shipping and handling

Available from the LYWA, Wisdom Publications (Boston), Wisdom Books (London), Mandala Books (Melbourne), Snow Lion Publications (USA) and FPMT centers everywhere. Discount for bookstores. Free for members of the International Mahayana Institute.

OTHER TEACHINGS OF
LAMA YESHE AND LAMA ZOPA RINPOCHE
CURRENTLY AVAILABLE

BOOKS PUBLISHED BY WISDOM PUBLICATIONS

Wisdom Energy, by Lama Yeshe and Lama Zopa Rinpoche
Introduction to Tantra, by Lama Yeshe
Transforming Problems, by Lama Zopa Rinpoche
The Door to Satisfaction, by Lama Zopa Rinpoche
The Tantric Path of Purification, by Lama Yeshe
The Bliss of Inner Fire, by Lama Yeshe

A number of transcripts by Lama Yeshe and Lama Zopa are also available. For more information about these transcripts or the books mentioned above, see the Wisdom Web site (www.wisdompubs.org) or contact Wisdom directly at 199 Elm Street, Somerville, MA 02144, USA, or Wisdom distributors such as Snow Lion Publications (USA), Wisdom Books (England), or Mandala Books (Australia).

VIDEOS OF LAMA YESHE
Available in both PAL and NTSC formats.

Introduction to Tantra: 2 tapes, US$40
The Three Principal Aspects of the Path: 2 tapes, US$40
Offering Tsok to Heruka Vajrasattva: 3 tapes, US$50

Shipping and handling extra. Available from LYWA, Mandala Books, Wisdom Books, or Meridian Trust (London). Contact LYWA for more details or see our Web site, www.LamaYeshe.com

What to do with Dharma teachings

The Buddhadharma is the true source of happiness for all sentient beings. Books like this show you how to put the teachings into practice and integrate them into your life, whereby you get the happiness you seek. Therefore, anything containing Dharma teachings or the names of your teachers is more precious than other material objects and should be treated with respect. To avoid creating the karma of not meeting the Dharma again in future lives, please do not put books (or other holy objects) on the floor or underneath other stuff, step over or sit upon them, or use them for mundane purposes such as propping up wobbly tables. They should be kept in a clean, high place, separate from worldly writings, and wrapped in cloth when being carried around. These are but a few considerations.

Should you need to get rid of Dharma materials, they should not be thrown in the rubbish but burned in a special way. Briefly: do not incinerate such materials with other trash, but alone, and as they burn, recite the mantra OM AH HUM. As the smoke rises, visualize that it pervades all of space, carrying the essence of the Dharma to all sentient beings in the six samsaric realms, purifying their minds, alleviating their suffering, and bringing them all happiness, up to and including enlightenment. Some people might find this practice a bit unusual, but it is given according to tradition. Thank you very much.

Dedication

Through the merit created by preparing, reading, thinking about and sharing this book with others, may all teachers of the Dharma live long and healthy lives, may the Dharma spread throughout the infinite reaches of space, and may all sentient beings quickly attain enlightenment.

In whichever realm, country, area or place this book may be, may there be no war, drought, famine, disease, injury, disharmony or unhappiness, may there be only great prosperity, may every thing needed be easily obtained, and may all be guided by only perfectly qualified Dharma teachers, enjoy the happiness of Dharma, have only love and compassion for all beings, and only benefit and never harm each other.

LAMA THUBTEN ZOPA RINPOCHE

Rinpoche was born in Thami, Nepal, in 1946. At the age of three he was recognized as the reincarnation of the Lawudo Lama, who had lived nearby at Lawudo, within sight of Rinpoche's Thami home. Rinpoche's own description of his early years may be found in his book, *The Door to Satisfaction* (Wisdom Publications). At the age of ten, Rinpoche went to Tibet and studied and meditated at Domo Geshe Rinpoche's monastery near Pagri, until the Chinese occupation of Tibet in 1959 forced him to forsake Tibet for the safety of Bhutan. Rinpoche then went to the Tibetan refugee camp at Buxa Duar, West Bengal, India, where he met Lama Yeshe, who became his closest teacher. The Lamas went to Nepal in 1967, and over the next few years built Kopan and Lawudo Monasteries. In 1971 Lama Zopa Rinpoche gave the first of his famous annual lam-rim retreat courses, which continue at Kopan to this day. In 1974, with Lama Yeshe, Rinpoche began traveling the world to teach and establish centers of Dharma. When Lama Yeshe passed away in 1984, Rinpoche took over as spiritual head of the FPMT, which has continued to flourish under his peerless leadership. More details of Rinpoche's life and work may be found on the FPMT Web site, www.fpmt.org. Rinpoche's other published teachings include *Wisdom Energy* (with Lama Yeshe), *Transforming Problems,* and a number of transcripts and practice booklets (available from Wisdom Publications at www.wisdompubs.org).

DR. NICHOLAS RIBUSH, MB, BS, is a graduate of Melbourne University Medical School (1964) who first encountered Buddhism at Kopan Monastery in 1972. Since then he has been a student of Lamas Yeshe and Zopa Rinpoche and a full time worker for the FPMT. He was a monk from 1974 to 1986. He established FPMT archiving and publishing activities at Kopan in 1973, and with Lama Yeshe founded Wisdom Publications in 1975. Between 1981 and 1996 he served variously as Wisdom's director, editorial director and director of development. Over the years he has edited and published many teachings by Lama Yeshe and Lama Zopa Rinpoche, and established and/or directed several other FPMT activities, including the International Mahayana Institute, Tushita Mahayana Meditation Centre, the Enlightened Experience Celebration, Mahayana Publications, Kurukulla Center for Tibetan Buddhist Studies and now the Lama Yeshe Wisdom Archive. He has been a member of the FPMT board of directors since its inception in 1983.